A SECOND
CHANCE

ALSO FROM AFRICAN RIGHTS

Women Taking a Lead: Progress Towards Empowerment and Gender Equity in Rwanda

A SECOND
CHANCE

What Economic Opportunities Mean for

Impoverished Women in Rwanda

By Rakiya Omaar and
Elizabeth Ashamu of African Rights

rwanda
gift for life

African Rights documents human rights violations, investigates genocide and conflict and promotes dialogue. It focuses on countries scarred by violence, to highlight abuses and to bring the voices of victims and other concerned parties to the center of debates about how to secure rights. It brings a strong commitment to participatory research together with experienced advocacy.

Rwanda Gift for Life is a U.S.-based non-profit organization that supports women in Rwanda who were raped during the 1994 genocide and are now living with AIDS. The women and their children—some of whom are also HIV-positive—regain their physical and emotional health through access to medical care, essential nutrition, trauma counseling, education for their children, decent housing, and income-generating activities.

All photographs courtesy of Fair Winds Trading, Inc.

ISBN 978-1-60643-261-7

First published in the United States by Rwanda Gift For Life.

First edition

Designed by Jamie Kerner

10 9 8 7 6 5 4 3 2 1

Table of Contents

Acknowledgments

Rwanda Gift for Life and African Rights would like to thank Ted Waitt of the Waitt Family Foundation for the grant that made the research and writing of this book possible, and for his continuous interest and encouragement.

We also recognize Norm Waitt of the Kind World Foundation, Cindy Waitt, Durinda Aspleaf, and Lee Lysne for their generosity of spirit.

We would also like to express our gratitude to the staff of African Rights and to the interpreters who worked tirelessly to make this book a possibility: Georgette Kamaliza, Madeleine Yambabariye, Gyslaine Uwitonze, Félicien Bahizi, Gustave Mukurarinda, Yves Rwasa, Alphonse Rurinda, Fred Sserwadda, and Ezra Bitagwa.

Special thanks also go to Pascasie Mukaburigo, Celine Wambajimana, Irène Mujawayesu, and Pierre Nzeyimana, for their invaluable help in explaining the story behind weaving in Rwanda, and in facilitating contact with weavers.

Most important of all, we would like to extend our appreciation to the weavers and beaders themselves who gave so generously of their time. Most of those quoted in this report gladly extended permission for their names to be used. Some, for reasons of personal safety, gave permission to be quoted but asked that they not be identified; for these, we have provided (and noted) pseudonyms.

We hope that *A Second Chance* has done justice to the story of their struggles, achievements, hopes, and aspirations.

Acronyms and Glossary of Terms

ARVs   Anti-retroviral drugs used primarily to manage HIV/AIDS

AVEGA   Association of Genocide Widows of April

CERAI   Integrated Rural and Craft Center

CFJ   Youth Training Center

COOPAR   Cooperative of Rwandese Artisans

COVAM   Cooperative of Weavers of Mukingi

FARG   Fund to Assist Survivors of the Genocide

PPMER   Project for the Promotion of Small Rural Micro-Finance Projects

NGO   Non-governmental Organization

RIEPA   Rwanda Investment and Export Promotion Authority

Abunzi   Mediators in local disputes

Cellule   A local unit of government, the smallest in Rwanda's successive administrative units (cellule, sector, district, and province).

Gacaca   Courts established to try genocide suspects in locales where the crime took place

Igikoma   Porridge made of sorghum flour

Ikigage   A local beer made from sorghum

Indagara	A type of small dried fish
Inyangamugayo	Judges in *gacaca* courts
Kitenge	Wax print fabric tied around the waist used by women
Responsable	The head of a cellule
Sosoma	Flour made from mixed grains
Umudugudu	Low income housing projects
Urwaga	Locally brewed beer made from bananas

Preface

In 2004 Macy's, "America's Department Store," began selling stunningly beautiful Rwandese baskets. Terry Lundgren, Macy's Chairman, President and CEO, saw the baskets and heard the basket weavers' story as told to him by Willa Shalit, founder of Fair Winds Trading, a marketing and importing company that promotes economic development in Africa and elsewhere. As sales of baskets grew from a few thousand in 2004 to more than 40,000 in 2008, the number of weavers with products coming to the United States swelled to as many as 3,000.

The research behind *A Second Chance* was intended to explore what has happened in the lives of weavers as a result of sustained employment. The majority had only known intense poverty; many were survivors of the genocide or were living with HIV/AIDS. Until now, no one knew, in fact, the impact of basket weaving—the consequence of sustainable employment —on those most responsible for the work: the weavers.

The story that unfolds in the following pages was made possible by a generous grant from the Waitt Family Foundation to Rwanda Gift for Life, which commissioned African Rights, a human rights organization in Rwanda, to undertake the study.

Rakiya Omaar, Director of African Rights, managed and co-authored the study with Elizabeth Ashamu, a researcher at African Rights.

Introduction

A *Second Chance: What Economic Opportunities Mean for Impoverished Women in Rwanda* is an intricate and personal book that examines the consequences of gainful employment on Rwandese women by telling the stories of female basket weavers and bracelet beaders who produce high-quality crafts for export to the U.S. In the rural Gitarama and Butare regions of southern Rwanda, approximately 3,000 women, and some men, spend their days crafting baskets as members of various associations and cooperatives. This book is based on detailed and extensive interviews with nearly 100 of these weavers, and includes interviews with some of their husbands, as well as with male co-workers and trainers. A small group of women making bracelets from semi-precious stones live in the capital, Kigali, and their experiences of working in an urban context are also shared.

This book, funded by the Waitt Family Foundation, looks in depth at the economic and social impact of these two income-generating projects. These initiatives are the result of the inspiration and commitment of a U.S.-based company, Fair Winds Trading. It provides a unique insight into how employment as professional artisans has affected these women as workers, wives, mothers, and citizens. *A Second Chance* also outlines the broader effects of weaving on families and communities by considering to what extent the establishment of weaving and beading associations provides a platform to address and tackle, in a practical manner, social concerns such as poverty, HIV/AIDS, family planning, violence against women, and the community fissures produced by the 1994 genocide. Finally, *A Second Chance* illuminates the perspectives of the craftswomen on the challenges they face and notes their suggestions for the future.

This analysis is accompanied by a quantitative survey based on extensive interviews with 360 weavers which provides vital statistics over a broad range of questions about how their lives have been affected by becoming professional weavers, ranging from enrolment of children in schools, to changes in their diet, to accurate information about HIV/AIDS, to learning about laws that have been passed to protect women's human rights.

—RAKIYA OMAAR, DIRECTOR
AFRICAN RIGHTS

An Executive Summary

Basket weaving is enshrined in Rwandese cultural heritage as an important practical and recreational activity for women. Historically, mothers would be sure to pass on to their young daughters the knowledge of how to weave because an ability to shape baskets was considered a prerequisite to marriage. Particular talent was associated with being a good housewife. Baskets were used for domestic purposes, either as decoration or to store food, and were commonly exchanged between families and friends as gifts.

The nature of basket weaving has changed dramatically over the past few years as it has become an export business promoted by the Government of Rwanda and cultivated by buyers who have found international markets for Rwandese hand-woven baskets. The largest export market is in the U.S., and is a result of the partnership between Fair Winds Trading and Macy's, where the baskets are finally sold. Demands for higher quality from buyers abroad have spurred significant developments in the style of baskets and in the techniques, materials, and designs that are used.

As the economic rewards of basket weaving have become apparent in the impoverished rural communities of Rwanda, where there is little alternative to the harsh life of subsistence farming in the most densely populated country in

Africa, more and more men have joined women in basket weaving associations. A number of these men are former prisoners arrested as genocide suspects. They learned to weave while in prison, and formed their own associations, which included men and women, upon their release. A number have become very skilled weavers and train others, including genocide survivors, with whom it would otherwise be very difficult for them to interact.

Basket weaving's significance in modern-day Rwanda is seen in gainful employment producing positive results in many areas of the lives of weavers. Gender inequality and poverty are closely linked and, therefore, the changing economic situation of many women is leading them to greater empowerment within both their families and their communities. The women who are making bracelets in Kigali have been working for a much shorter period, but the strides they have made economically in just a few months is striking.

The Economic Implications

Weaving has had a tremendous impact on the economic well being of many women and their families in Rwanda. Of those interviewed, ninety-eight percent said their standard of living has improved as a consequence of their weaving and becoming members of a weaving association. The majority of these women either never went to school, or had completed only a few years of primary school before they dropped out because their families could not pay the fees, or because they were needed to help till the land. But now they can afford a better quality of life. This includes the ability to educate their children, to pay for healthcare, to eat a more consistent, balanced and healthy diet. Although weaving has meant that women devote less of their own time to the traditional occupation of farming, the income from weaving has allowed them to hire helpers to cultivate their fields. They have also been able to buy more land to cultivate or to pay for improvements to their property, expanding or building upon an existing structure. Many have also begun to save money, either in a bank account or through the cooperative. They find it easier to get credit from local shopkeepers, or loans from the weaving association or from the bank.

The women agreed unanimously that the family benefits more directly from a woman's income than from the money earned by a man. The men interviewed for this book agreed with this conclusion. As the women are able to provide more adequately for their family and to better focus on their families' needs, children are cleaner, better dressed, and better educated. Women can now afford to pay for books, uniforms, school fees, lamps for studying in the evening and, where necessary, supplementary evening classes. The children eat a healthier and more balanced diet, which helps them concentrate and to be successful at school.

The women themselves are more presentable on a day-to-day basis. They can afford basic items such as soap, oil, toothpaste, fabric, as well as products viewed as "luxury items" like sanitary napkins. Instead of cultivating in the fields, the women often meet with each other to work, and they have a sense of pride in being well-presented.

Standards of health among weavers and their families have clearly improved: Forty percent more weavers have medical insurance than in the past. The fact that they can also buy fresh milk, fruit, and vegetables on a more regular basis also contributes to a healthier life.

In the past, it was unusual for poor women in the countryside to save money as most did not work, or worked as subsistence farmers on their own land, which did not generate much of an income. But weaving and beading have enabled a lot of women to open back accounts or save with the cooperative. Fifty-two percent of weavers now save more than before they started to weave, and those who do not have savings accounts use methods like rotating funds, or purchase large amounts of beans or sorghum to store and sell when the prices for these items are high.

With the money comes a feeling of independence, and the knowledge that they are now contributors to the family in their own right. These women no longer see themselves as a burden on their husbands, and speak of feeling responsible for the family's welfare as a whole, rather than being limited to household chores.

Poverty, in any society, creates a web of dependency on the resources of relatives, the charity of neighbors, and handouts from non-governmental organizations or state institutions. Because employment opportunities for women in the Rwandese countryside have always been few and far between, those with no income inevitably relied on communal solidarity to move those around them to extend their own meager resources. What the women now treasure, above all else, is that they are able to stand on their own two feet, and that the wider community also benefits.

The Effect on Personal Relations

With their newly found independence, many married women said that they now have more say in the decisions that affect their family. Some went further and added that they feel a greater sense of respect from their husbands, which has strengthened their relationship as a couple. This is particularly marked in couples where both are weavers. Many husbands are proud that their wives are raising their family's standard of living and can report tangible benefits that the income from weaving has brought.

The Social Consequences

Working together in a group gives women a support network that provides them with an arena in which to have discussions, ask questions, and share emotional and practical problems. There are more women who can visit them when they are sick, or lend them money when the need arises. Being with others has opened up their minds to new ideas, which, together with their new economic reality, has made them more optimistic about the future. This, in turn, gives them confidence that extends to other areas of their life.

Because they are more confident and independent, the women who have become weavers are more likely to become involved in local government and public affairs. Weavers are better dressed and cleaner than other women in their neighborhood, which carries a great deal of weight, especially in rural communities. Many have traveled to meet government officials or buyers, which exposes them to new people and ideas, all of which broadens their outlook.

Through their associations, weavers and beaders are discovering more about HIV, mainly by talking to each other. Many of the women and men are themselves HIV-positive, and they encourage their fellow workers to go for testing, to talk to their partners, and to practice safe sex. Increased financial security also means that those who are infected can afford the healthy diet that will enable them to remain on an ARV (anti-retroviral) regimen, and to buy medication for opportunistic diseases.

Economic instability often goes hand-in-hand with dependency on men, and this is all too common in Rwanda. Many women feel that financial necessity compels them to compromise themselves and their children, but weavers (and beaders who produce jewelry) can take care of their own needs. The associations also provide women with an opportunity to learn about family planning and birth control. Women not only talk about these issues at work, but sometimes take the new ideas home and share them with their husbands.

CHAPTER I

From Individual Art to an Export Business

HOW BASKET WEAVING CHANGED IN RWANDA

The practice of weaving has deep roots and significance in Rwandese culture. For centuries, both men and women have intertwined grasses, reeds, and plant fibers to create products that serve functional and ornamental purposes. The current and past uses of woven products are numerous: Floor coverings, wall hangings, living structures, bedding, plates, and containers have and continue to be crafted with woven natural plant materials.

Among the many varieties of woven products, baskets hold an honored place. With infinite shapes and designs, baskets serve as decorative, practical, and symbolic objects. They are sometimes works of art, intricately detailed with abstract geometric motifs. Other times they are produced out of necessity, for storage of grains, or in their finer forms, for holding precious objects such as jewelry or money. They are also used for wrapping gifts, or storing food stuffs like beans and maize. They may be used as plates for foods known locally as *posho* or *bugari*. Some are props in Rwandese dances. Following wedding ceremonies, brides enter their new homes with baskets filled with food to supply them through their first weeks as wives. As gifts exchanged between families and individuals, baskets are symbols of friendship and love, and sitting on the tables and atop shelves in almost every Rwandese home, they are said to bring good luck, wealth, and abundance.

Baskets have been part of the traditional ceremony called *Gutwikurura,* "Uncovering the Bride," and are given to the girl by her parents as gifts while other baskets are used to carry various gifts to the new couple. Baskets given at marriage are meant for decoration in the house and in the wedding hall, or during any traditional ceremony.

For women, particularly those in rural areas, weaving has been not only popular but, according to Anatalia Niwemutima, a weaver in the Huye district, it has been a rite of passage.

> *It was considered a woman's responsibility to instruct girls in weaving. The main role of a mother was to prepare her daughters to be mothers and wives by setting an example for them. Weaving is a part of Rwandese culture. Before receiving a marriage proposal a girl needed to be a perfect house wife and this was measured by how much she wove and how well. The importance of weaving was mainly domestic; baskets were used to store foodstuffs like beans and as decorations. Elders also used small baskets for keeping their money, especially coins.*

Given their variety of uses and importance in daily life, baskets have always been considered valuable objects. For a long time, however, their use was primarily domestic and local. But over the years, baskets have gradually become important commodities, first within Rwanda and now internationally. Basket weaving has shifted from being a hobby exclusively for women to an economic activity, a profession sought out by both women and men. Weavers who worked alone in their homes now gather as groups and have formed structured cooperatives. Innovations in design and developments in form have heightened the beauty and perfection of this ancient craft. Such evolutions in practice and purpose, traced through this chapter, build a context for how baskets have become international export products.

The Abahuje of Gitarama

In Ruhango district, in a region commonly known as Gitarama, members of a cooperative of weavers called Abahuje dedicate their days and weeks to crafting brilliantly colored fruit bowls. By sewing sisal fibers around blades of sweet grass, they slowly build concentric coils and stitch them around and around to form a slightly rounded bowl. They weave as their primary profession and earn income by selling their baskets.

In days past, while women in this area made baskets principally for personal domestic use, they could also barter or sell their products. Gitarama is dry and cultivation is difficult, so selling baskets, even on a very small scale, provided useful cash for a population consisting primarily of subsistence farmers. Séraphine Nyirafurere described the weaving she observed as a child.

When I was in primary school, I had aunts who wove using grasses from the valley to make traditional baskets called ibyibo. *They used them to store sorghum and beans, and they would also sell them. Traditionally, we'd make baskets for storing things, and to use in the house. Sometimes we'd even eat out of baskets. We didn't have pots, pans, or plastic so we used woven materials as much as possible.*

Baskets were made because they were needed for practical reasons, rather than for sale. Weaving was seen as an activity for girls, and it kept them occupied. Weavers woke up early and were busy; they didn't have time to waste.

As a young mother and elementary school teacher, Catherine Bwinturo, now seventy-seven, would make the same simple hand-woven open-topped baskets, the *ibyibo*, in her spare time.

Everyone in Rwanda knew how to weave then, even if they didn't know how to weave very fine things. All girls would learn how to make ibyibo *when they were young. You couldn't get married without knowing how to weave and make* ibyibo. *In addition to teaching, I used to make* ibyibo *baskets and I sold them.*

According to older weavers like Séraphine, a convent in Save, Butare (the first Catholic parish established in Rwanda), developed the skills of local women and taught them to weave more refined and intricate baskets, helping to take weaving beyond functional household products.

Many years ago, some nuns in Save taught embroidery, sewing, and wall decorations to young girls who had finished primary school. Then they taught us how to make baskets from banana fibers and string, using needles. When the girls got married and moved away, they helped to spread weaving across Gitarama.

One crucial step towards making baskets a commercial commodity was the shift away from using fibers from the trunks of banana trees to using sisal. Séraphine recounted that Silesian monks in Kimihurura, Kigali, who purchased baskets from Gitarama, especially encouraged this particular development.

In order to give our baskets more value, these white monks advised us to use sisal to weave rather than banana fibers, saying the banana fibers spoiled quickly. So we started to make baskets using sisal. As we knew how to weave with the other materials, it wasn't difficult for us to change materials.

Sisal fibers, extracted from the thick green branches of sisal plants that grow across the Rwandese countryside, are strong and bright white. They take dyes easily, and with them women could form sturdy and durable baskets while expanding the browns and blacks of nature's color palette. Catherine was among the first women in the area to learn how to make sisal *uduseke*.

When my husband died, my former students told me that I had helped them so much and they didn't want me to suffer and live in poverty as a result of his death. One of them thought it would be a good idea for me to develop my weaving, and so he took me to meet with Mama Miriam, a nun at the Save convent. The nuns there knew how to weave with sisal and so I went and I learned from them how to make sisal uduseke.

It was in only in the late 1970s when weaving in Gitarama began to take hold as a significant and widespread economic activity. The convent at

Save, and particularly Sister Miriam, provided an accessible market, which further motivated women to weave. Eugenie Nyanzira took up weaving when she was sixteen and her parents, who were farmers, did not have the money for her to continue studying. She remembers taking her baskets to the convent around this time.

> *Sister Miriam started purchasing baskets. We'd make series of* uduseke *and sell them for between 500 and 1000 francs. Back then, this was a very good price. Money had much higher value than it does now.*

The first sisal weavers, like Catherine, taught others and gradually knowledge spread among women in the area.

> *My neighbors saw me weaving and were excited, so they started to learn from me. I'd prepare the sisal for them and teach them. I did this all for free. Weaving spread from woman to woman. We taught many girls, and if one got married, she'd move, and then teach other girls in her new area. This is how weaving spread throughout Gitarama.*

The proximity of Gitarama to Kigali facilitated the expansion of weaving in the area. Women were able to seek out buyers in the capital. Catherine and Séraphine became businesswomen, purchasing baskets from craftswomen in the area and traveling to Kigali, often on foot, to sell their wares there. Catherine described how she served as an intermediary.

> *After women finished their baskets, I'd collect all of them and transport them to Kigali. Transportation then cost fifty francs. But sometimes, we couldn't find a car and we'd have to walk all the way to Kigali. We'd go as a group of about four and we'd help each other carry the baskets. When I reached Kigali, I'd go to the airport in the morning to sell baskets. A set of five* uduseke *was 400 francs. We always made* uduseke *in sets.*

Eugenie made these sets of nesting *uduseke*, five baskets gradually descending in size so that they could be enclosed within each other. She gave them to Catherine to sell in Kigali.

We sold our baskets to some female entrepreneurs who had buyers in Kigali. Catherine was one of them and I was her client. We were paid about 200 or 250 francs for a small series of baskets.

The creation of a cooperative of weavers called COVAM (Cooperative of Weavers of Mukingi) was a first step towards the organization of weavers and of basket sales. Founded in 1977, it joined approximately thirty weavers and businesswomen together. Catherine was among the founding members, along with Séraphine, who currently serves as the cooperative's president. Séraphine spelled out the founding principle of this cooperative.

Our goals were to be economically self-sufficient and to teach others how to weave. We especially targeted young girls who had left school, so they could have a way of making money and not become maids or street children.

Soon after it was created, COVAM linked with another new cooperative called COOPAR (Cooperative of Rwandese Artisans), which helped ensure the weavers of COVAM that they would have a market for their baskets. COOPAR was created in 1979 by group of fourteen businesspeople and artisans from across the country, who came together to open a store in Kigali that would sell a range of craft products purchased from artisans in Gitarama, Kigali, Butare, Ruhengeri, and Kibungo. Both cooperatives continue to pool efforts to link with buyers in Rwanda and sometimes export internationally.

The opportunity for rural women in Gitarama to weave for, and deliver their baskets to, these cooperatives gave rise to the proliferation of professional weavers in the area, as well as female entrepreneurs who would oversee the buying and selling of the baskets. Séraphine commented that "before working in the association, women didn't like to weave that much."

Sometimes they'd weave and sometimes not. But with the association, they saw that they could make money. And as members, they motivated each other.

From the 1970s onward, weaving came to be seen as a profession. It was an activity that women, particularly young girls and widows, turned to for supplementary income. The weavers crafted and sold their products; baskets criss-crossed the country through networks of businesspeople, associations, and cooperatives.

The partnership that has been at the heart of the export of baskets from Gitarama was forged in 1996 when Janet Nkubana met Irène Mujawayesu, commonly known by her nickname, "Dukuze," hawking baskets on the streets of Kigali. Janet and her sister, Joy Ndungutse, had founded Gahaya Links, a handicraft production and sales company. Dukuze, Catherine's daughter, had weaving and commerce in her blood.

I've been in this business for a long time. I used to follow my mother to buy baskets from women in the village and sell them in Kigali. We would meet different clients interested in purchasing baskets, and that's how I met Janet in 1996. Janet started to buy from us and send the baskets to the U.S. Janet liked the baskets very much. She increased the order and even began to specify the type of baskets she wanted.

In 2003, when Gahaya Links entered into business with what is now Fair Winds Trading, weavers in Gitarama were called upon to increase production dramatically. Eugenie was one of the women who benefited from this development.

Dukuze brought Janet and [her sister] Joy into our area for the first time in 2003. For the series that I made, I earned 3,000 francs. Janet and Joy urged us to make a lot of baskets. Many weavers were attracted by the prices they were offering.

Given the large number of women ready to go to work, and the quantity of baskets on order, Joy and Janet encouraged the weavers to create better structures in order to work more efficiently. Joy explained this process.

We realized they were disorganized, so we started to group them. We told them to form small, tighter groups, with leaders who were literate and master weavers to manage each team.

With Dukuze as president, Abahuje, meaning "The United," was formed in 2003. This cooperative now includes approximately 1,600 weavers, who are organized geographically into groups of twenty to thirty people. The groups assemble several times a week under trees or in small production centers to weave together. The weavers of Abahuje are the principal suppliers for Gahaya Links. They deliver and sell their products once a week, and are paid regular and fixed prices. From Gahaya Links, the baskets are sold to Fair Winds Trading who oversees their transatlantic voyage to Macy's.

In addition to their organization and structure, Abahuje's products and skills have also evolved, through constant innovations in product design and development, and periodical skills training sessions. Dean Ericson, the president and Rwanda representative of Fair Winds Trading, attributed this shift to a team effort between Macy's, Fair Winds Trading, Gahaya Links, and the weavers themselves.

It has been a lot of work to get the baskets to look as they do now. We've changed many details and improved the finishing. This cost a great deal of time, effort, and money. Now we have a great product and we can change the colors and design as much as we want. It's durable, it's stackable, and it's practical. Before, the product was made in the village and then someone tried to find a market for it. Now, things go in the opposite direction. The market determines the product that's made in the village.

Catherine has been a weaver for more than fifty years, giving her a broad perspective as she reflects on the changes in style and quality.

When I started to weave, we only wove in black and white as these were the only colors we had. But now there are many colors, like blue, red, and green. Also the designs have altered. We only used to weave traditional Rwandese designs, but these days the weavers are adopting designs that have come from other countries. This is good; it means the women have developed because of these new styles.

Vestine Mukeshimana echoed her enthusiasm for these innovations.

We are using different materials, new styles and dyes. In addition to sisal, we now also have raffia from Uganda. Before, we didn't think of using materials from outside.

Gahaya Links strives not only to cultivate the weavers' artistic skills, but also their business savvy. "We've taught the groups," said Joy, "about quality, delivery time, and bookkeeping."

Through training, they learned how to keep records for paying workers and saving. We've formed a team of master weavers, and we teach them the new designs developed by our creative team. We teach them about delivery management and set them timetables. We teach them about colors and dyeing. We develop our own trainers among the women.

The Weavers of Peace Baskets

A few hours south of Gitarama lies Butare, Rwanda's second-largest city, where the sectors of Rusatira, Ruhashya and Rwaniro in Huye district are home to several cooperatives by the names of Dufatanye ("Shared Work"), Ubumwe ("Unity"), and Dukundane ("Mutual Love."). These weavers gather in small groups, dispersed across the hills. They craft intricate *uduseke*, cone-topped baskets made with papyrus, sisal, and banana fibers that have come to be known as "peace baskets." Portrayed at the center of Rwanda's seal, these baskets have become prominent national symbols. As in Gitarama, baskets in Butare have made a similar journey from treasured objects of use and exchange among Rwandese to commodities produced in bulk and sent abroad for sale.

In Rwanda, it is impossible to escape the history and lasting effects of the genocide and, especially for these cooperatives, the carnage of 1994 is a key element in how their story has unfolded, and in how weaving caught on in Butare. At the source of the immense skill and talent flowing through the weavers in Huye are Pascasie Mukaburigo, a genocide survivor and widow, and Antoine Ntaganda, a convicted genocide perpetrator.

Pascasie Mukaburigo founded the weaving cooperative, Abishize Hamwe (meaning "The United"), whose members gather at a center in Kinkanga, a small commercial hub in Rusatira sector. Pascasie currently holds the position of vice president. She began weaving in 1959 when she was fifteen, and although she could create many things, she most enjoyed shaping baskets. She described her weaving in those days as primarily a hobby.

Weaving for us was a pastime. We made baskets for decoration and for gifts and also because it was fun.

While Gitarama weavers looked to Kigali for a market, with her father's help Pascasie sold baskets to European doctors working at the hospital in Butare, located just south of where she lived. These sales were only occasional, but when a national museum opened in Butare, and bought the craft items of local artisans, Pascasie also began selling there. As an experienced weaver and a budding entrepreneur, she decided to form an association of weavers in the 1970s.

I taught many people to weave and some of my students became master weavers. The name of the association then was Abishize Hamwe ("The United"). I had to look for a market within Rwanda, but I also wanted to sell to foreigners. My father had contacts with some Americans and Europeans, and so when they came, they would sometimes buy our baskets. Before the genocide, there were also some outlets, mostly in Kigali, that purchased our baskets, such as ASPAR in Gikondo, Caritas, and La Finesse.

Consolée Mukaremera, forty-four, was one of the early members of Pascasie's association in Kinkanga.

I began learning how to weave when I was a child of about fourteen or fifteen. Pascasie was my neighbor. She first assembled a group of women weavers and later founded an association. I would go and visit her where she and the other women wove together. I watched her weave and started to learn through observation. I gradually acquired experience. I decided to start making baskets because I knew weaving would help me to earn money. I became a member of the association because Pascasie, the president, was the only one in the area who knew where and how to find buyers for the baskets. I didn't know who bought them or where they were sent. Others also joined the association to make a profit. In those days, Pascasie purchased the baskets for 120 francs.

Odette Mukamanzi was also a member and decided to pass the knowledge of weaving on to her husband. Although men wove mats, ropes, and other materials, baskets were considered exclusively a women's vocation.

Antoine Ntaganda, perhaps the first male to embrace basket-weaving as a profession, explained why he took up the art of weaving in 1981.

I wasn't happy being just a farmer, and I thought it would raise my standard of living. It was something which wouldn't interfere with my farming. My wife, who had learned from her sister, taught me. We wove together in Pascasie's group. I was the first man to become a weaver as it was considered a woman's job. But other men subsequently became interested. When I finished a basket, I sold it in Butare or Kigali. Sometimes I gave them to Pascasie to sell for me.

Pascasie remembered Ntaganda as "one of my first weavers. He learned from one of my students."

The 1994 genocide tore apart communities across Rwanda. Pascasie's group of weavers was no exception, as Consolée underlined.

Some died and others fled and went into exile. And because of what happened, there was hatred between people. The members who were still around no longer met up.

Some of the members joined groups of armed militiamen in committing violence, including Ntaganda, who admits that he played a role.

I participated in the genocide of 1994 and I was given a thirty-year sentence by the gacaca court of Gashoba, in Ruhashya. I was found guilty of taking a direct part in the killings.

That April, Pascasie was in Kigali; she had gone there to sell baskets. She hid in the Catholic Parish of Sainte Famille in central Kigali. Her husband and many of her children and grandchildren back home in Ruhashya were not so fortunate. She returned to Ruhashya in August 1994.

People, including members of my association and some who had killed my relatives and looted and destroyed my house, were afraid to confront me. I lost my husband and several children and grandchildren. I have three children who survived. Many of the women who had woven with me were dead. It was an extremely distressing time.

Gradually, Pascasie found seven women who were willing to start weaving once again.

These were women who had been married to Tutsi men and they had all lost their husbands and children. These were the only people who would come and speak with me.

At first, there was no market for the baskets. They wove, Pascasie commented, "as a way of passing time and for the chance to meet up and chat."

After the genocide, this was very important. Weaving together was also a way of attracting other women to join the association. Gradually, other Hutu women who had had Tutsi husbands, Tutsi survivors and Twa women, and then eventually women whose relatives had participated in the killings, all started to become members of the association.

She gave an example of the intimacy of the violence, and of the courage it took to agree to work together.

There is a woman called Ancilla who is one of the weavers with family members accused of killing. She joined the association in 1998. It took time for her to come and work with us because her husband murdered one of my husband's daughters.

Consolée, widowed in 1995 during the forcible break-up of the Hutu refugee camps in Kibeho, Gikongoro, was among the first women to take up weaving again beside Pascasie.

Pascasie made efforts to unite us again, but many were afraid to approach her. They thought she was plotting to find a way to take revenge against them. Despite these rumors, a small group decided to go with her. We were the foundation of the new association and slowly more people came to us. I knew Pascasie was a good woman. I knew what had happened to her and to her family, but I wasn't afraid of her. She had done so much for my family and she was my neighbor.

Pascasie's message further won over Consolée.

I was also convinced by what she said. She told us that if we continued to distance ourselves from her, we would never be together again. She said it was better for us to join her so we could all work together, build trust in each other and, by being truthful and honest about what happened, renew the unity of our community. Then, as people started to see us weaving side-by-side, others came on board.

While women in Kinkanga were weaving, Ntaganda, imprisoned in Ruhashya, began, in 1999, to share his knowledge of weaving with his fellow inmates accused of genocide crimes.

I taught approximately 300 people. Many were then transferred to Nyanza and Mpanga central prisons where they in turn taught other prisoners. By bribing some prison guards, we were able to sell our baskets to Pascasie for about 3,000 to 4,000 francs.

François Ntambara from Huye was among Ntaganda's students in prison. He started weaving in 2002, at first "just to learn something new."

But afterwards we began making money because there were buyers. In prison, we got very little money for the baskets. The most I'd make was 1,500 francs for one agaseke. *No one told us who bought them. I used the money for clothes and I'd send some to my wife to use for food and for visiting me. Weaving helped me in prison and this is why I came to like it.*

When Ntambara and other prisoners were released, they brought their skills to their communities and taught those who wished to learn. When large numbers of prisoners were being released, particularly after 2003, they established weaving associations and cooperatives in their home areas. Cyprien Hakizimana, released from a jail in Ruhashya in 2005, helped to set up a cooperative in Rwaniro of which he is now president.

Some officials asked me to train the local residents, and so I founded Dukundane. There were weavers who already had some experience, but who weren't working. I trained them and that's how the cooperative started.

Dukundane now sells peace baskets to Spéciose Brown, a businesswoman who in turn supplies them to Fair Winds Trading. Spéciose has also formed a small group of weavers in Samuduha, Kigali.

The Ubumwe cooperative in Ruhashya sector was also an initiative of former prisoners, including Tharcisse Kaberuka, who was freed in 2005.

I began with my wife and my children. The association started with fifty people, and grew. We are now about seventy in Mara, and we hope to go on growing.

I taught others because I saw that weaving was a useful activity. I knew that it had brought money to us as a family. And also, as an association, we could make more baskets and earn more money.

AVEGA, a national association of genocide widows, serves as a buyer for the Ubumwe group and an intermediary between them and Fair Winds Trading. The Dufatanye group in Rusatira sector, which currently has two hundred members, also weaves for AVEGA.

In Kigali, Women for Women International, a non-governmental organization (NGO), began teaching women to weave in the first half of 2007 as part of its economic skills programs for poor and disadvantaged women. New to weaving and still undergoing training, this small group of women is just beginning to supply peace baskets to Fair Winds Trading.

Access to a regular market was key to the strength and numbers of these groups and cooperatives. Françoise Mukagihana, a businesswoman, was the first to connect the weavers in Ruhashya to Fair Winds Trading and Macy's. The existence of an international market, she said, had immediate consequences.

The women used to estimate the size of the basket. But to export, we had to teach them to make the baskets all exactly the same size, with new and different designs and flawless quality.

Selling to Macy's, she added, was "a good experience."

It forced us to improve the quality of our products. We also learned how to better organize ourselves, as we had to produce the required number of baskets at a specific given time. And because the order was large, this was especially good for the women. Basket weaving became an everyday activity that they could rely on economically. The export of handcrafts in Rwanda is evolving. I have seen substantial progress in the quality of the weavers' work.

Based on critical reviews from American customers who had purchased the baskets, Dean Ericson has worked with his various suppliers to continuously improve the structural design of the peace baskets.

People wrote on the website that the [peace] baskets didn't sit straight, that they were flimsy and that the tops didn't close. We had to come up with a new and improved version. A woman called Agnès Nirere made a hard peace basket. When I saw this, I was really impressed. The way the bottom and top edges are finished on Agnes's basket was much nicer. She is a brilliant craftswoman. Also, we want to include the weaver's name in the basket to present it as a unique handcrafted work of art, signed by the weavers. Americans will appreciate this. So there are a number of new innovations that we've made to this basket.

From a Pastime to a Profession

When asked to name their profession, women did not hesitate to respond "weaver." Indeed, as if they were working hourly office jobs, many begin weaving in the morning and continue until the evening, pausing only for a quick break at lunch. They weave five days a week or more. It is clear that what was formerly a leisure activity is now a job. Pierre Nzeyimana, the AVEGA income generating projects coordinator, is the main liaison with the weavers in Huye. He attributes this shift to the fact that weaving is increasingly lucrative.

Because women no longer see weaving as a hobby, but as a means to sustain their families, they now spend the whole day weaving, and treat it as a profession.

Pascasie wants the women to see what they do as a profession, in order to foster dedication and pride in their work.

*I tell them to look upon weaving as a serious profession, to regard their work
in the same way that they regard teaching or nursing.*

Joseline Kanyange, a twenty-three year-old weaver in Ubumwe
cooperative, has gained understanding of the national significance of baskets
and of weaving through the radio.

*I have heard our President on the radio calling upon all Rwandese, especially
women, to get involved in making udeseke. He says there is an international
market and that they are an easy source of income. The importance of baskets
in our culture was decorative, but today they have become more commercial.
We all weave because we want to make money out of it.*

Spéciose Mukamugenzi, from Mara in Ruhashya, was similarly
persuaded.

*Today, people weave because they want to make money. And we hear the
government praising basket weaving.*

A new feature is that weaving is now sought out by both sexes.

*As you can see, there are so many men involved in weaving. Actually, they are
the best weavers, trainers, and initiators of the new basket forms.*

Séraphine says the export of quality baskets has helped to make Rwanda
better known internationally. "The baskets have gone international, and
made Rwanda a feature on the world map of craft making." Angelique
Dusabe, a young weaver, also sees that basket weaving has become a key
element in visions and plans for national development.

*Baskets have become a source of income for so many weavers. I always hear
leaders, including the President, speaking on the radio, urging us to learn
weaving and telling us that this is crucial to our development.*

Indeed, the Rwandese government has taken numerous initiatives to
support and promote basket weaving as well as the production of other
handicrafts, and sees potential in the development of this sector. As a

land-locked country with no mineral resources, Rwanda's economy relies principally on agriculture and the export of coffee and tea. Anxious to expand the export of its products, Rwandese artisans receive considerable backing through the Ministry of Commerce, the Private Sector Federation, the Rwandan Investment and Export Promotion Agency (RIEPA), and the Project for the Promotion of Rural Small and Micro-Enterprises (PPMER). Basket weavers have benefited from training in cooperative formation and management, the funding of training workshops, the construction of handicraft production centers, and the facilitation of contacts with potential buyers. Much more than simply a national symbol, baskets are perceived as a key to prosperity.

CHAPTER 2

Acquiring a Skill

LEARNING TO WEAVE

Today there are approximately three thousand weavers involved in crafting baskets professionally in the districts of Ruhango and Huye in southern Rwanda. Associations of predominantly female artisans include both younger and older women, beginners as well as master weavers. Each has a unique story of how, and why, she was drawn to weaving, and these tales are key to knowing and understanding the women who form the cooperatives.

Throughout Rwanda, people are increasingly being taught to weave through structured training sessions, often funded by NGOs or the government. But in Huye and Ruhango, where weaving is so deeply entrenched, the skill is continuously passed on informally from person to person, and cooperatives grow spontaneously and organically. From mother to daughter, from older to younger sister, between relatives and neighbors, and also from former prisoners to women in their communities, one by one weavers are initiated into the art of producing baskets as their ancestors have done for generations.

Common to the women weavers are the desire to improve their quality of life and the hope of gaining financial stability and comfort through weaving. As they speak of the factors that lead them to spend hours sitting over baskets, the challenges that have marked these women's lives are all too clear. Many cite poverty, widowhood, landlessness and illness as the conditions that push them to weave. Others speak of being forced to become financially independent at young ages and of looking after their parents, children, and relatives. They turned to weaving out of need. Given their low level of education, and living in rural areas where economic opportunities are limited, weaving is seen as one of very few options for earning income. In Huye, an additional impetus was the clear evidence that weaving was profitable when they saw improvements in the living standards of families whose men were weaving from prison.

And there is an additional factor at work for many: the beauty of the work and of the baskets themselves.

Weaving in Response to Poverty

Alphonsine Mukamugema learned to weave in the 1960s as a young girl "because culturally, all women and girls are supposed to weave." She sold small baskets for one hundred francs each. At her age, this was "big money," which gave her the incentive to hone her skills and keep weaving. When she married, making baskets took up her free time. Then came widowhood and the needs of her own three children, and those of three children of her late sister who are in her care. Weaving has become her economic lifeline.

> *My husband was poor, so my weaving supplemented his income and made it possible for us to buy things like salt and soap. My husband's death was a huge setback because it meant I was on my own. My oldest child did well in his primary school exams and so I needed money to pay for his high school education. Weaving became work that could help me.*

Economically, women in Rwanda generally rely on their husbands' income. As a result, widows find themselves facing difficulties on many fronts. Providence Mukamusonera, thirty-three, lost her husband in 1996. Since then, she has continuously struggled to raise her two young children. She normally works as a farm laborer, though even that is not guaranteed because it is seasonal work.

As a laborer, I make 350 francs a day. My rent is 1,500 francs a month. I don't have any land. It's hard for me to pay the rent and find money for food. My children are in school, but I don't have money to pay for school materials. People in the community, including the teachers, take pity on us. My poverty is no secret; everyone in the community can see it for themselves.

Her neighbors in the Byimana sector of Ruhango suggested weaving as a solution. The Abahuje weavers welcomed her warmly, and one of her neighbors gave her some sisal for free. A lack of options made Providence a fast learner.

I've finished and sold one basket. I was given 2,750 francs for it. The other 250 francs went to the association. I used the money to buy food.

When she looks at the other weavers, Providence is hopeful that weaving will alleviate her constant financial concerns.

Weavers are better off than others, especially those who are experienced. Their economic situation is superior to people who don't weave. I know one weaver called Jeanne who used to be like me, but you can't compare us anymore. She looks after her three children, lives in a nice house and hopes to build another. Her children are doing well in primary school. You just have to look at them and you can see that they are more healthy. She is also able to save.

Also living in Byimana is Marie-Claire Mukeshimana, who took up weaving in only her third year of primary school.

I had older sisters who wove and they taught me how to make small agaseke. I'd make baskets and give them to my sisters. They'd sell them to Dukuze's mother and give me money, which I used to buy things for myself. We also had an aunt who we sold to.

Even as a child she thought of weaving as "something that could help me support myself and pay for my primary school." She finished primary school and after one year at CERAI (Integrated Rural and Craft Center), family circumstances pushed her to spend more time crafting baskets. She was living with her grandmother who had broken her leg, and Marie-Claire was asked to stay at home to look after the cows and build her knowledge of weaving.

Because weaving requires little physical exertion, those who are ill, weak, or unable to cultivate see it as an alternative occupation. Yvette (a pseudonym), thirty-five, is married and has three children. She discovered she was HIV-positive in 2002 and started weaving three years later with the hope of gaining an income. The fact that a number of her neighbors were weavers with Abahuje and had done well out of it was also an important consideration. The idleness of the dry season gave her the time to consider weaving.

When we aren't cultivating, we don't have anything else to do. I used to like sitting with weavers, so I asked them to teach me.

Azelle (a pseudonym) was taught how to weave by her sister when she was twelve and in her fifth year of primary school. The next year, she failed to pass the state exam that would allow her to continue her studies at no cost. Her father had left her mother to marry a second wife, and her mother, who had to care for Azelle and her siblings, had no money for school fees. So Azelle became a talented weaver at a young age and, because she knew how to write, she could weave words into her baskets, and these intricate designs added to the baskets' value. She sold hers to Catherine and Dukuze, and earned "quite a bit of money." By pooling their earnings, Azelle and her older sisters were able to build a house for their mother.

Azelle married a wealthy businessman at eighteen and no longer needed to weave. She divorced him because he was unfaithful, and married her second and current husband, Marc, in 1988. But Marc's own infidelity led them both to contract HIV/AIDS. They learned of their condition in 2001 and Azelle took up weaving again and joined Abahuje in 2002. Marc explained why.

Life was difficult. Because I didn't have land, it was hard for us to buy any animals. With her weaving, we were able to take care of some of our needs.

With only one young child at home, Azelle's income enables her and her husband to live comfortably, maintain their health, and to adopt a positive outlook.

Anatalia Niwemutima is originally from Huye and learned how to weave when she was thirteen. After she married and moved to Kigali, she stopped weaving. But her husband was a victim of the 1994 genocide, and she herself was so badly beaten that she needed an operation and had to undergo hospital treatment for two years. With assistance from various NGOs, she managed to look after her two children, pay her hospital bills, and even start a small business. But this eventually failed and she was desperate for a solution.

I sat down and thought about what I could do, and my mind went back to the weaving I used to do. I started weaving again in 2000. My doctor had advised me not to do anything that would require a lot of energy from me.

Even with her permanent physical impairments, Anatalia is now an instructor in the Women for Women peace basket program. Like many others, weaving was the answer she found in her time of need.

Weaving after Primary School

In Rwanda, six years of free primary school education is guaranteed for all, but at the end of this period, when they are on average thirteen years old, students take State exams that determine their future course of study. Only those who pass the exam can continue on to public schools, where their families pay approximately sixty dollars a year in tuition fees. Those unable to pay often receive assistance from the Ministry of Education or NGOs that step in to cover the costs. But those who do not pass the exam must either repeat the previous year and retake the exam to gain admission to a State school, or enroll in a private school for which their parents will pay more than twice the State tuition rate. Since many families, particularly those in rural areas, cannot afford private schools, they tend to remove their children, especially girls, from formal education at the end of primary school.

At thirteen, when many leave school, young girls are old enough to be useful to their families at home, particularly in working the land. Depending on their family's situation, many are expected to strike out on their own and become economically independent of their parents. But with few employment opportunities and a level of education that will not open doors, some move to Kigali to work as maids. Others marry early. Increasingly, young people are turning to weaving to gain independence and income, as Catherine Bwinturo remarked.

Here, when children finish primary school and can't go to high school, they don't go to the youth training center to learn how to sew. They would rather stay at home and learn to weave. There are also some boys who have started to weave.

Some of the baskets Catherine has sold were made by Aristude Mukashyaka, who took up weaving after primary school. Said Aristude:

My mother, who liked to weave, taught me since I didn't have a job. My mother then took my baskets to Dukuze's mother.

In the past, Aristude wove wall decorations. Now at thirty-three, she is president of the Kibanda group in the Abahuje cooperative. She has woven sets of three black-and-white baskets with a pattern in the center that only the most focused weavers are able to make.

Eugenie Nyanzira, like Aristude, failed the State primary school exam and subsequently stopped school. She approached some girls who lived near her and asked them to teach her to weave.

I thought weaving would change my economic prospects. In the past, a child living at home couldn't be independent as she had no way of earning money. But those who could get money without asking their parents could buy nice dresses that they themselves had chosen. We only got a little bit of money for weaving, but enough so that I could also buy nice dresses or skirts. My parents were supportive. I was the only girl in the family and the youngest. They saw that I liked to weave and was really motivated, so they would sometimes contribute to the money I earned so that I could buy new clothes.

Only twenty, Julienne Uwambajimana is new to the cooperative. Near the end of her sixth year in primary school, she fell ill with a urinary infection and missed the national exam. When she recovered, she decided to not return to school to repeat the year, especially as her parents, who were farmers, could not pay for her schooling. Although she is the youngest in her family, Julienne wanted to give a helping hand to her parents. She considered going to Kigali to work as a maid, but chose instead to emulate her older sister, a weaver.

Monique Mukamana's small income filled important needs for her parents and siblings.

I started weaving when I was still in primary school, and took it up seriously once I had finished primary school. I sold ibyibo *baskets for 200 francs each to buy simple things for my family, like soap or salt.*

At fifteen, Séraphine Mukandamage, a resident of Ntenyo in the Byimana sector, completed primary school and began producing baskets "to reduce my poverty."

I joined the cooperative in 2002 because I knew that I couldn't become a better weaver on my own.

Now the mother of six children ranging in age from fifteen to three, Séraphine was also attracted by the savings and credit plan that the Abahuje cooperative has for its members.

I was interested in saving because I have many children who are still young who will need to go to school.

Abakunda Umulima, which means "Those Who Love Work," is the name of Claudine Uwiragiye's small group of weavers in Nyakabuye cellule in Byimana. For her, having cash to purchase small personal items made her want to learn how to weave.

I started weaving in 1989 after primary school. Our mother used to encourage weaving so that we could buy soap and hair oil. I learned weaving from a neighbor and from my mother, who were both perfect weavers. I used to watch them weave. Then one day my mother helped me start a basket to learn on. It wasn't good enough to sell, so we used it at home. The next basket was nice and we sold it. My mother bought me hair gel with the money which made me really happy. From then on, I continued weaving.

Claudine became a member of Abahuje in 2004.

I saw most of my neighbors were members and were making good money out of weaving. Weaving is expected of a Rwandese woman, but it also helps women who did not go to school and have no jobs to have an income.

For the Beauty of Baskets

For some women, their interest in weaving comes, first and foremost, from the beauty of the craft and the joy of weaving. Vestine Mukeshimana began weaving when she was only seven, and against the will of her parents.

One of our neighbors had many daughters who liked weaving. I loved to watch them and I learned from them. My parents didn't like me weaving because it meant I ignored the housework.

She found weaving "a nice and fun activity."

It was just something that I enjoyed doing. But I saw that weavers had neat houses, decorations on the walls, and tablecloths. Their homes were tidy and comfortable. So I also started weaving because I wanted to be like them.

Vestine began making sets of *uduseke* when she was twelve and used the money to buy clothes and lotion. Now twenty-six, she weaves multi-colored fruit bowls.

Athanasia Mukayandwi dropped out of school when she was eleven to care for her ill mother. Her sister, who is mentally ill, cannot work. At twenty-two, she has many responsibilities and there are clear financial reasons why she would want to weave. But Athanasia was drawn in by the finesse of the work and the grace and intricacy of the baskets. She started in

May 2006 and makes *uduseke* with the Ubumwe association in Ruhashya sector, Huye.

> *My mother made ordinary baskets for use in the house. I joined the association simply because I like the way they weave the baskets.*

She keeps some of the baskets at home "just to look at them and admire them."

> *I think that they are so beautiful.*

Help From Unexpected Sources: Liberated Prisoners

Many women in Huye district learned weaving from prisoners who were detained as genocide suspects and taught weaving while imprisoned. After being separated from their communities for up to thirteen years, ex-prisoners returned to their homes with a valuable skill they were eager to share with others. Local authorities encouraged these men to pass on their talents and they tutored their neighbors free of charge. The improvements they brought about in their own families through weaving served as advertisements to others about the potential benefits of selling baskets. There were also financial incentives: They knew that with larger numbers of weavers, they could better attract buyers. Some have taken on the role of businessmen and serve as intermediaries between the weavers and those who purchase the baskets.

When released, they first taught new weaving techniques to their mothers, sisters and wives, and then taught others in the community, sometimes actively seeking out women. Jean-Baptiste Rucahobatinya, released in 2003, never attended school but with other former prisoners helped found a weaving group in the Ruhashya Ubumwe cooperative.

> *At first only two or three came, but now we have more than one hundred members. Other freed prisoners and I couldn't do anything else because this was the trade we had learned in prison. We thought it was important to train others so they could develop themselves.*

People were eager to weave because of the income it brings. When we get 8,000 francs for a basket, we can solve many family problems. And weaving isn't a tiring profession. We work sitting down and can combine this with other work. For example, sometimes I pause to go and look for grass for the cow. And for the young girls, when they want powder or cosmetic products, they normally can't afford them easily, but now they can.

On leaving prison, Jean-Baptiste lived with his cousin, who is the husband of Godansi Mukabahizi. He wove in the house and Godansi would watch him work; she began to learn from him in July 2006.

I saw that the baskets he made were different from the ones we were used to weaving. That's how I got interested in them. I first practiced on his baskets and later on he bought me my own frame. He would start for me and I'd continue weaving. After he saw that I was making good progress, he asked me to join their association.

In 2005, Jean-Baptiste taught his stepmother, Costasie Uwambaye, who also lives in Mara and who, before weaving, was a farmer. Jean-Baptiste's younger sister is twenty-four and has a young child. She is separated from her husband and weaves, thanks to her brother's training. The chain of weavers that Jean-Baptiste has formed is exemplary of how other prisoners have taught their female relatives and friends.

Dévota Kabahire, twenty-four, was first attracted to weaving by the situation of the prisoners' families.

When they were in prison, they gave baskets to their wives [to sell]. Even though the men were in jail, their families lived better than we did.

"Their liberation," she said, "was an important day in the community." She began to weave in 2004, when she became their student.

Jeanne D'Arc Murekatete began making *uduseke* baskets two years ago under the tutelage of two former inmates, Akimana and Martin.

They used to teach weaving by the roadside on my way home. So when I was ready to learn, I approached them. The fact that they had been prisoners never bothered me. I saw that others were learning from them and that they were teaching for free.

When she was young, Anatalia wove baskets and mats for domestic use. She would cultivate her fields and work in other people's farms for 300 francs a day, far from adequate to sustain her and her family. She is a widow and has three children aged eighteen, nine, and six.

In 2005, I heard that there was a specific basket on the market and wanted to master it. Claude Twagirayezu, a released prisoner, mobilized and taught us to weave this new type of agaseke. My first basket wasn't great, so I didn't sell it. Twagirayezu was responsible for selling and seeking out markets.

Through a Training Course

The weavers on which this book focuses learned to weave primarily through informal networks. Today, nationally, it is becoming more and more popular for the State or for NGOs to sponsor training programs to teach new weavers, especially those living in areas where weaving is not as historically rooted.

Gahaya Links has a training center (funded in part by the Kind World Foundation) in Kicukiro, Kigali, where they train women how to weave with the goal of equipping them with a skill that will allow them to earn an income. The women spend several weeks at the center learning to make baskets. Africare is paying for Esther (a pseudonym) to stay at the Gahaya training center. She arrived with nine other members of an association in Rwamagana, Kibungo, called Kwizera, which joins people living with HIV/AIDS and their caregivers. Esther is the adoptive mother of a sixteen-year-old orphan who was diagnosed as HIV-positive two years ago.

Africare wanted us to do this training so that we could learn more about weaving. I was happy to come because I know that it's always good and beneficial to learn how to make new things. I enjoy weaving. I just finished making a wall hanging. I think that people will come and buy our products, even though we aren't very experienced.

Esther hopes that she will leave Gahaya Links' training program with knowledge that will help her gain an income to better support and educate the young girl in her care.

Chapter 3

A Better Quality of Life

The Economic Implications

Weaving has had a tremendous impact on the economic well-being of women and their families in Rwanda. Ninety-eight percent of those interviewed said their standard of living has improved as a result of weaving and becoming members of a weaving association. Before they started weaving, many artisans in rural areas felt entrenched in poverty, with few opportunities to emerge from lives where they worried daily about where they would find food and cash to provide for basic needs. But for most, weaving has broken this cycle. As each payment represents the hours they spend leaning over their baskets, the weavers control their earnings with care and use them judiciously, to improve their families' quality of life. They are gradually climbing up the socio-economic ladder from being hired workers and landless peasants to subsistence or even commercial farmers and livestock keepers. The income generated by weaving has allowed women to buy or rent more land, and to hire helpers to cultivate their fields. Paying for their children's school fees and materials is no longer a struggle. Many have also begun to save money, either in a bank account or through their cooperative, and they find it easier to get credit from local shopkeepers, a cooperative, or the bank. These economic implications mean that women, regardless of their age or marital status, can feel independent and stand on their own feet.

As other craftswomen, Aristude sees her occupation as the only answer to so many urgent needs.

Besides weaving, there is no other way for women to make money. We ask ourselves how we would survive if we weren't weaving.

The First to Benefit: The Family

With wives and mothers becoming the primary breadwinners, weavers have noticed a shift in how household resources are spent and managed. Many said that when money is placed in a woman's hand, her immediate thoughts are how she can most effectively use it to the advantage of her family. Neither male nor female artisans, nor their spouses, could say the same about cash in the hand of a husband or father. Indeed, men and women agreed that the income a woman earns will certainly benefit her family more directly than income earned by a man.

Espérance Mukandutiye, a weaver from Nyakabuye, Gitarama, gave this explanation for why women appear to spend more of their money on the family.

The man doesn't know in detail all the things the family needs. But the woman, who looks after the house, is aware of everything that is missing. Also, after the man is paid, he may go out and drink a lot. He starts by saying that he wants just one bottle, but before you know it, he's finished all the money. But when I'm making money, it benefits our home more than when it's my husband who's earning the same amount of money.

There is a strong culture of drinking beer in Rwanda and every small community has a house-front bar selling local banana and sorghum beers, known as *urwagwa* and *ikigage*. Théodore Rutagengwa, whose wife is a weaver, agrees that beer is one item that drains men's income.

Men spend their money on things that aren't important for the family. For example, if the wife makes 1,000 francs a day, the whole 1,000 is used in the home. But the husband won't bring all it to the house. I'm not even sure that he'd bring home 500 francs. He'll go and buy a drink because the first thing he thinks about is his thirst. In the evening, he'll buy potatoes for 300 francs, then he'll get thirsty again and use the rest of the money on another drink.

Rwandese community bars are not only for drinking; they are also meeting places for men and serve as their primary arenas for socializing. Offering a friend a drink or interacting over full glasses is a social convention that is sometimes hard for men to escape. Pascal Munyemana, married to an Abahuje weaver, spoke from experience.

Say someone gets a long sentence in gacaca. *The other men want to sympathize with him and comfort him and say that things will be okay, so they take him to the bar. Or, say a man has just recently been released and comes back into the community. We have to welcome him with beer. This is how men's money can be spent, with no planning and on things that have nothing to do with the family.*

Pascal concluded by admitting that women's money, on the other hand, "is all spent on things that we need at home." The fact that "women plan" is one reason why Théodore says money is better spent by his spouse.

My wife can say that she's going to buy this and that, and she won't spend money on anything else.

Pascal readily admitted that when he was working as a construction worker, "things were completely different."

Unless men are forced to follow rules about spending their money, it will take a long time for them to act differently. I try to tell other men to use their money as women do, but this isn't easy.

Joseph weaves with his wife, but has learned the advantage of entrusting both of their incomes to her.

My wife is more aware of the children's needs than I am. She knows who needs new clothes and also how many days of payment we owe our hired cultivators. I always know how much money there is, but normally, it's my wife who keeps it.

Joseph is convinced that putting revenue in the pockets of women is the best way to promote general development.

Weaving brings incomes to both women and their families. If you want to impact the family as a whole, empower women because they have a heart for the entire family, as well as for the community.

New Ways of Getting By

In rural areas of Rwanda, because agriculture and animal rearing are the primary activities by which families support themselves, access to land and possession of livestock provide clear indicators of a family's financial situation. Landless or near-landless peasants working as hired laborers sit at the bottom of rural economies. Families with access to land through inheritance, purchase, or rental are a significant step above the landless. Moving upward along this scale, families shift to cultivating not only for subsistence but also for sale of produce, employing workers on their land, and rearing animals for profit. Although many weavers still struggle to make ends meet, all have begun to take steps to emerge from the worst forms of poverty, and these shifts—from scratching out survival, to coping easily and building up assets—have deep significance for rural Rwandese families.

Land in Rwanda is precious and scarce. Many have no land, or not enough to cultivate and provide their families with staple food products. Landless women and men live in the constant routine of tilling others' land in the hope of making enough money to feed themselves, but rarely much more. In the regions of Gitarama and Butare, a day of farm labor can fetch from 300 to 500 francs, and these workers have no assurance of finding a steady stream of work. The dry season, during which there is a pause in agricultural activities, places landless families in an even more desperate situation. Unable to save or invest, hand-to-mouth poverty is nearly impossible.

Many of the men and women who now spend their days crafting baskets describe themselves as having risen from among the most destitute in their communities. Three-quarters of those interviewed said that before weaving they had no source of income. With weaving, they have employment that raises substantially the amount of cash entering their homes. Weavers making fruit bowls with the Abahuje weavers of Gitarama earn an income two, three, or four times greater than they were previously making, resulting in significant shifts in the comfort in which they live.

At fifty-two, Spéciose Mukamugenzi, a weaver in Mara, Huye district, is relieved to avoid hard physical labor and make peace baskets for increased revenue.

I used to work on peoples' fields for only 300 francs a day, just to buy soap and salt. This kind of work required a lot of energy, but the returns were miserable. I had to put in so much effort, yet the money couldn't help my family. With weaving, I don't have to toil away digging, and I make relatively good money.

With an income of at least 1,000 francs a day, Costasie Uwambaye pointed out that weaving more than tripled the income of a hired laborer.

Dévota observed that the increase in cash makes families of weavers "better off than those who don't weave."

For example, a good weaver can earn 8,000 francs a week. But someone who doesn't weave can earn 400 francs a day for farming. That's 2,000 a week, and a simple cultivator may not even have regular work.

As a significantly larger sum of money begins entering their homes, weavers first look to investing it in their families' agricultural production through purchasing or renting land and hiring farm workers. One third of rural weavers are now able to rent some land, and thirteen percent say they have bought plots. Espérance and her husband do not have much land of their own, but for the first time her income from weaving has allowed them to add to the area that they can cultivate. They pay 5,000 francs a year for this extra field.

Although they are not growing enough to make profit from sales, Yvonne and her husband have increased the amount of staple food products such as beans, sorghum, bananas, and sweet potatoes that they can use for their own consumption. Her husband can concentrate his labor on their own crops, rather than just hoping to find work caring for plants that will feed another family.

Azelle is another weaver who has directed money from basket sales to renting land.

I am renting one field in Ruhango, but I plan on renting three more. I also rent three fields in the valley where we cultivate sweet potatoes.

With too much land for her husband to cultivate on his own, she now pays for others to work alongside him.

When I started weaving my husband stopped going around looking for work to make money. Now he takes care of the farming activities, the house, and the fields. I can hire people to cultivate for us and my husband oversees them.

With land and hired workers, Azelle can boost farm output to the point that her family has the possibility of producing a surplus and the option of offering some for sale to earn extra income.

We grow cassava, rice, or sweet potatoes, and sometimes when we have enough, we can sell some.

Stephanie Yankurije is fortunate because her husband, as a construction worker and carpenter, earns 20,000 francs a month. Their incomes complement each other; while his earnings bought cows, hers helps to feed them. Stephanie's basket money goes towards supporting agricultural activity in several ways.

We use my money to buy materials and tools for cultivating, seeds from the market, and sometimes to pay someone to help cultivate.

A widow, Consolée Mukaremera sees a great importance in her ability to hire workers. Rather than working in the fields herself, she devotes herself to weaving. She does not purchase food, but looks to the earth surrounding her home in Gashoba cellule.

With my earnings, I pay for people to come and farm my land. This is as if I was purchasing food, but I think that it's better for me to invest the money into making the land produce.

"There's been progress," commented Dévota on her farming activities since she began weaving.

With weaving, I can be sure that I'll have money in a short time, and on a regular basis. I can improve on our agricultural production because I can pay people to work on the farm.

Where land is the primary source of life, Rwandese relish resources extracted from their hills. Having long experience with drought and erosion, they recognize the reality that cultivation has its risks and irregularities. Dévota made the point that farming does not generate much profit, and is relieved that she does not need to rely on it for income and sustenance. "My life now cannot compare to my life before I started weaving," she said.

Between planting and harvest, you have to wait three months. And even then, you can't be sure that the crops will succeed. I used to be miserable. Everything depended on agriculture. I couldn't buy anything.

Once they have access to arable and productive land, Rwandese strive to save money to purchase and raise small animals like goats, pigs, and chickens, which provide compost to fertilize fields and are another source of food for a family's consumption. Small animals also produce offspring that can be offered for sale and are assets that can be taken to the market in the event of an emergency or urgent need for cash. Forty-three percent of the weavers say that they have bought animals since weaving, including Dévota, the proud owner of two goats.

Since we had no money, I couldn't have dreamed of owning them before.

Emmanuel Musengimana, from Mara, used to farm anywhere he could find work for 500 francs a day. But weaving, he said, "has made me prosper more than farming." Able to take care of his family's basic necessities and step in should there be a poor harvest, he also puts money aside to "invest in productive things like goats, pigs, and chickens."

I have acquired three goats, two pigs, and five hens since I started weaving.

When Vestine Mukeshimana gave birth to her youngest child, she didn't have enough money to pay hospital fees. But she did have a pig she had purchased with money from weaving.

My family sold the pig to pay for my healthcare. I've since bought a rabbit and now I'm planning how to buy more animals. I want to buy a new pig because pigs reproduce easily and I can earn a profit from selling the piglets.

Carefully managed income allowed Josephine Mukantembe to introduce an animal to her home in Nyakabuye, Byimana.

I bought a pig by saving 1000 francs a week. A small pig costs 5,000 francs.

For some, like François Ntambara, acquiring livestock still seems like a distant possibility.

When I get money, it goes from my hand to my mouth. I need it to feed my family. I have two children, twelve and ten, and our land is small and not fertile. I don't even own it; I rent it for 5,000 francs a year.

Owning a cow is synonymous with wealth and comfort for rural families. In addition to manure that enriches the soil, cows provide milk, which can be sold daily to bring a new and constant source of revenue. Tharcisse Kaberuka and his wife weave together, and their combined income has both given him the hope of purchasing a cow and reinforced his self-confidence.

There's a big difference between weavers and others. My wife and I can make at least six baskets each month. That gives us 40,000 francs, which is the same as some State employees. So, even though I'm a simple farmer, I'm at the same level as teachers. With this money, I can now project into the future and know that I'll soon be able to buy a cow because I know that I'll make money. But what can a simple farmer project for the future?

Azelle first bought a goat and a pig, and almost has enough money for a cow.

Yesterday I sold a pig for 10,000 francs. I had 30,000 before that and now I have 40,000. I'm planning on buying a cow in the future. I'm nearly there.

Owning a cow also remains an aspiration for Athanasia.

If the weaving work is permanent, I'll be able to get many things. For example, I'd buy an animal so we can have fertilizer and milk.

If she can obtain credit, Costasie has her eyes set on buying a cow and going into business.

I could buy different items and sell them when they become less available and the prices go up. Each person has his own ideas and strategies for earning extra income.

Dévota certainly has her own ideas.

I buy sorghum and beans when they aren't expensive and store them at home. Then I sell them when they become more costly. I've bought 200 kilos of beans. It is not yet the moment to buy sorghum, but I plan on buying 200 kilos of this as well. I bought the beans for 200 francs a kilo, and will sell them for 350 francs per kilo. The sorghum I bought at 100 francs per kilo, and I'll sell this for 200 francs a kilo.

Tharcisse Kaberuka is also planning to diversify his sources of revenue, saying that he has paid for membership in a rice cooperative.

What is evident is that weavers now have the means to afford not only basic necessities, but a range of items that they would previously have considered prohibitive "luxury items."

Material Possessions

Weaving has brought something new to rural families: liquid cash. Before they began weaving, when the only possible ways to obtain cash were by working as paid laborers or selling produce, not many saw money pass through their hands in the course of a week or even a month. Now, a steady influx of Rwandese francs into the local economy has changed the purchasing power of families with weavers, allowing them to acquire many more material possessions.

"Weavers," observed Stephanie Yankurije, "get money easily and regularly."

Non-weavers wait for their husbands to come home with money. And when finally there is money, they have a long list of things. When these families harvest, they have to empty their house out to make cash. But weavers get money and can keep the food at home, and purchase what they need.

Stephanie no longer considers lamp oil, soap, and clothes as beyond her reach.

Joseline Kanyange, twenty-three, said her husband is supportive of her weaving because he sees what it contributes to their home. She earns much more than his average monthly income of 8,000 francs, and her revenue allows them to avoid selling food to purchase household goods.

In a month between 16,000 and 20,000 francs comes into my hands. Before weaving, we used to sell some of our produce to afford household necessities like soap and salt. Now, I use the money from weaving to buy all of these things as well as clothes, shoes, flour and tomatoes.

A single mother, Jeanne D'Arc Murekatete is delighted that can buy clothes for herself and her seven-month-old child. After she has paid the people who cultivate for her, she takes pleasure in knowing she can buy what she called "girl things" including soap, lotion and, she said, especially sanitary napkins, which "keep you from getting embarrassed in front of other people." She can also wear shoes on a daily basis.

Weaving helps me a lot. Before I didn't always have shoes, and if I did, I'd have to save them for special occasions and couldn't wear them every day. But now I can buy shoes with my money.

Sitting in Ruhashya among a group of fellow peace basket weavers, Costasie pointed to some young craftswomen wearing T-shirts and skirts.

Take for example these young girls here. As cultivators they couldn't buy nice bright clothes like the ones they're wearing now.

She then spoke for herself and other older women who wear colorful wax print lengths of fabric around their waists, called *pagne* in French and *kitenge* in Kinyarwanda, "without sweating so much for them." Espérance no longer has to "wait for a long time before getting a new pagne."

Vestine's husband cultivates their land in Kamusenyi cellule, Byimana, but it does not yield them cash.

Our money, the 3,000 francs I make each week, comes from weaving. I buy soap, salt, and oil, the fundamentals for every family but which you can't get unless you are making baskets. Then it is clothes or other things.

Cyprien Bayingana is not surprised that families are sending their daughters to train with them in Rwaniro.

People notice that you've bought your wife a new dress without having to take anything to sell at the market, or that your child has a new uniform while others are sitting and waiting for their pigs to give birth.

Most weaving groups and cooperative presidents have mobile phones, which they need to communicate with their partners at AVEGA or Gahaya Links. In the past, the nearest telephones were in the closest commercial center, so when she sees a weaver with a phone, Alphonsine Mukamugema is impressed.

Weaving has brought development to our areas. Our leaders have telephones, which help us as an association and as a community. When there is emergency and we need to call somewhere, they always call for us for free.

Claudine, who belongs to the Abakunda Umulima group in Nyakabuye, confirmed the benefits of communication in the more remote areas of the country.

Through weaving, we have been able to get access to communication facilities in villages. All our presidents were given free phones which are useful to all of us. When you need to make an urgent call to Kigali, you just borrow one.

A member of Abahuje for four years, Aristude has a difficult time imagining life without the possessions that weaving puts within her reach.

A woman who weaves can buy clothes for herself, in any style she wants, and clothes for her children. She can also even buy clothes for her husband when he doesn't have money. At home, we can buy salt and oil and materials for cultivating. My life before wasn't good. Things are better now. I bought myself a phone and paid for it myself. If I weren't weaving, I couldn't go to the hair salon or buy clothes. If I wasn't weaving, my life would be bad.

Aristude went on to describe the visible differences between the homes of weavers and those who don't weave.

The homes of non-weavers aren't clean, they aren't cemented and usually they don't have an enclosure. Weavers have nice houses with cemented floors and a fence around them.

Based on Azelle's description, there is no comparison between entering the home of those who weave and those who do not.

The homes of weavers are stocked with many materials like cleaning supplies, lotion for the baby, kitchen utensils, and clothes. Also, sometimes weavers can afford to have a houseboy or girl. Some have been able to cement their floors or paint their doors.

Théodore gave further examples about the differences in housing.

Families with weavers are clean and don't have to put up with poor housing. They have different materials at home. For example, they can have two washing basins and none of them sleep on grass; they have mattresses. And they live in homes with cemented floors.

Such material purchases carry great significance in the lives of weavers and their families. As having soap and new clothes indicate that one is clean, maintaining good hygiene, and looking presentable, a cash income helps make immediate visual displays, differentiating weavers from non-weavers. Comments from the artisans reveal that their cleanliness and neatness also carry social and psychological weight, giving them the feeling of being "smart" or "happy."

Stephanie drew a sharp contrast between the children of weavers and non-weavers.

The children of weavers are cleaner than the children of non-weavers. Families without any weavers may spend up to week without any soap. But weavers never lack soap. And if one week you don't have money, you can buy it on credit. Weavers can also buy good clothes for their children.

"A sense of well-being" is one comfort that Dévota has derived from her basket revenue.

I can buy oils, beauty products, and things that girls need. I like the fact that I can dress well.

"Proud" is how Julienne feels. She completes one fruit bowl a week, which she sells to Gahaya Links for 3,000 francs.

Now I'm clean, I dress well and I can resolve simple problems at home. People respect me and think that I'm smart. When you look nice, you feel proud. Can you imagine how you feel if you don't have soap or clothes?

For Grâce Mujawamariya living in Byimana, the fact that weavers "look very presentable" was one of the reasons that motivated her to train as one.

In villages, it's really difficult for women to get good new clothes. But as a result of weaving, women have been able to buy themselves good clothes.

Even more important than clothes is the fact that weavers are eating much better than before, and much better than their neighbors who are non-weavers.

Diet and Nutrition

Changes in agricultural production as well as access to steady cash income have impacted weavers' diets in terms of both the quantity and diversity of the foods they eat. No longer forced to sell what they produce, many weavers keep more of the staple starches and cereals from their land for their families' own consumption. They have money to purchase foods that they don't grow themselves, allowing them to eat a more balanced and varied diet. As vitamins and minerals are essential to the health of adults and children, fresh fruit, vegetables, meat, and dairy products are necessary for staying fit and strong. More than three-quarters of the weavers eat more than they did prior to weaving. This improvement is one reason why Athanasia remarked of those stitching peace baskets around her in Mara, Ruhashya, "Families with weavers live comfortably."

Séraphine, the president of a small group of weavers in Ntenyo, is mother to six children between fifteen and three years old. They are all glad that they can eat things other than just the staple Rwandese starches.

My family's diet has improved. My children know that if I come home with money, I can buy them bread, igikoma *(porridge), or* sosoma *to make porridge rather than just using sorghum, or fruit. Or maybe I can buy them the small dried fish known as* indagara. *The children like all of these things. We eat meat on special occasions. This is another nice thing that I'm now able to offer them. But families with no weavers…can go many months without eating meat. Their children eat routine things like beans and sweet potatoes all the time. Because of weaving, I can say that this week I'll buy two kilos of sugar and porridge, and next week I'll be able to buy meat.*

It is because the money is in the hands of women, argued Séraphine, that it has a direct impact on the way their families eat.

A man won't think of giving extra money to his wife for fruits or vegetables. But women know the importance of these things and will buy them if they can. Fruits and vegetables are good for children and for everyone's bodies.

Eating beef or goat is considered a luxury for rural Rwandese families, but 26.3 percent of weavers said they now eat more meat. For Spéciose's family, "meat was a very rare meal." Costasie also said that "before weaving, I couldn't buy meat."

But now it's a little easier. Because we already have sorghum, sweet potatoes, and beans at home, we can sometimes consider buying meat. With weaving, we can eat meat every three months.

Aristude "no longer dreams of eating rice and meat."

I can now actually buy these things. We don't only eat sweet potatoes and beans. I can buy sugar and drink tea. I don't like milk, but other weavers can buy milk. I eat meat three times a month.

Before weaving, women could not fit eggs, another good source of protein, into family budgets, as eggs cost about one hundred francs each. But Stephanie notes that she is now able to give eggs to the three children in her care, as well as fruits like passion fruit and oranges.

Dévota supports her two younger siblings.

I can buy better quality food now and I have more selection. I can buy rice, potatoes, meat and vegetables. Before, I just ate sweet potatoes and some vegetables that I'd grow or find around the area. Now I can eat fruit, but before I couldn't dream of this. Really, I've noticed a huge improvement in our health.

The connection between an improved diet and better health, noted by Dévota, is significant, as is the money from weaving that makes basic health insurance affordable.

Healthcare: Giving Families a Future Together

With high prevalence and death rates from malaria, tuberculosis, AIDS and other diseases, having accessible and affordable healthcare is extremely important to families in Rwanda. The ability to obtain medicine when sick can often make the difference between living and dying from contracted illnesses or accidents. Each member of the family is vulnerable, and it is with this in mind that many weavers see that paying for healthcare insurance is worth the investment. A system of community-based health insurance plans called *mutuelle de santé* allow rural communities to access healthcare. By paying a per capita yearly subscription of 1,000 francs per person, individuals receive membership cards that allow them to visit the local health center or district hospital and receive subsidized care and medication, with only a small co-payment. These costs continue to be insurmountable for many Rwandese, but for weavers and their families, *mutuelle* is now something most can afford. Among the weavers, 86.66 percent now have health insurance and, of these, more than half obtained it since they began weaving. Despite these successes, one must also consider the fact that 13.33 percent of the weavers do not have insurance, either because they can't afford it or cannot make it a priority in their spending budgets.

Julienne, from Buhoro, Ruhango, came to understand the value of health insurance when she got sick.

> *We didn't use to care whether we had* mutuelle *or not. But then after I got mine, I got sick and was able to have healthcare without spending a lot of money. I explained this to my parents and so we decided that they should get* mutuelle *as well.*

Costasie learned the importance of having healthcare coverage the hard way.

> *Once, we all had malaria and didn't have the money to go and get treated. We bought pills, but divided them between us, and so the malaria became very serious.*

This bout of sickness left her children permanently weak, fragile, and susceptible to illness. Since then, even when working as a hired laborer, she did all that she could to pay for insurance.

Although my income was small, I made sure that we were able to pay mutuelle *because my children get sick often. We started paying* mutuelle *for 2,500 francs and then it increased to 3,000. And to get 3,000 when there was virtually no income coming into the house was difficult.*

Affording the yearly insurance premiums is now "much easier" for Costasie.

With money from weaving, we can pay for mutuelle *and have money left over to pay for food. Our health has improved. Things used to be so difficult, but now they're okay. I can rest.*

It is clear that for Aristude, the risk of falling ill does not have to be a source of financial anxiety.

I have mutuelle *and so does everyone in my family. I've found that my health has improved because I have insurance. Even if there's a moment when I'm uninsured, I know that I'll always have enough money to go to the hospital to be treated. And when I'm sick, I can buy porridge to help myself recover.*

When asked about her healthcare expenses, Consolée Mukaremera shrugged off the question as a concern of the past.

Now I pay yearly for health insurance. It's 5,000 francs a year for me and my four children, and a total of 6,200 francs including the cost of the prescriptions.

Some weavers, like Spéciose, have to single-handedly support relatives with chronic illnesses.

My husband has been sick for twenty-one years. He's mentally ill and sometimes becomes very unstable. The money I get helps me to take him to the psychiatric hospital in Butare every month. Without the money from baskets I think that by today he'd be wandering around. Instead, he is at home. So I am the only source of income for our family.

Alphonsine complains of persistent headaches, but they do not prevent her from leading a normal life.

Money from weaving has helped me to get treatment and drugs from Ndera Psychiatric Hospital. Without this I would be in mental distress.

When his child had an accident, although insurance covered most of the costs, François Ntambara had to use up his savings for co-payments and other related expenses. Now, when his family's yearly subscriptions are about to expire, he is confident that he'll renew them.

This is something I make a priority and struggle for.

With five children and so many other expenses to cover, Gisèle is among the women who have yet to join the *mutuelle* system.

Education: Hope for the Next Generation

Education is a gateway to a better life and although many weavers were denied this opportunity, they are keen that their children should not suffer in the same way. They talk of their desire to see their children complete primary school, and most have aspirations that their children will finish high school and go to university as well. While these ideas were once dreams, basket revenue helps to make them a reality. The children of weavers stand out from other children in a number of ways. Not only are they better dressed, but they are also healthier physically because they have a more varied and nutritious diet, which has had a profound effect on their ability to concentrate and perform in school. Children also have the tools to aid their studying: books, pens, paper, and even lamps so they can complete schoolwork in the evenings.

Eugenie Nyanzira, a mother of five from Byimana, underlined the critical contribution that the income from weaving has made to the advancement of education.

Weavers don't have any problems getting school materials or uniforms for their children. The children come to school regularly. You can see the differences between them and the children whose mothers don't weave. These children sometimes don't have materials or they don't come to class at all. It's often the families of weavers who give the other parents jobs that allow them to pay for their children's school fees.

Most families in the area cannot afford to pay for their children to attend high school level. This, however, isn't the case for weavers, who can afford to do so, or can at least take loans in order to send their children to high school.

Thérèse Mukangarambe, who weaves with the Abahuje association in Gitarama, has five children aged sixteen, fourteen, twelve, nine, and seven, who are in primary school. She pays 32,000 francs a semester in high school fees for her twenty-year-old. She asked a pertinent question.

My oldest child is in high school only because I'm weaving. Where would I find the money otherwise?

For children, coming to school without the correct books and supplies is discouraging and gives them little hope that they will excel. After their mother died, Dévota's younger siblings continued their schooling but often skipped classes because of shortages of materials. She has seen their enthusiasm grow once she made sure they had everything they need.

Now their attendance is regular and their grades are getting better. I'm hopeful that they will go to high school. This would make me happy. If they do go on to high school, I'll be able to pay, thanks to weaving. I'm so proud because I feel like I can play the role of both parents.

By boosting their morale as well as paying for supplementary classes, Séraphine's basket income also fosters her children's success.

The children of non-weavers sometimes don't have sugar or their parents can't pay for evening classes. But we weavers can afford all of these things. Weavers' children are happy. They know that if their mother sells a basket, she'll be able to do something special for them.

Girls cannot be professional weavers and students at the same time. But some, like Aristude's sister, find time to finish a few baskets over the course of the year, and can make a valuable contribution towards their own secondary school fees.

My younger sister is in senior two of high school. She weaves during her vacations and so she can make some money. She makes baskets and I sell them to Gahaya Links. She wouldn't be able to pay for all of her school fees on her own because she can't weave and study at the same time. If I wasn't weaving, I doubt that she'd be able to go to high school.

Passing the national exams at the end of primary school and thus gaining entry to public high school used to determine whether a student could continue his or her studies. Stephanie thinks that her children may continue, regardless of how they do on the exam.

I'll have money to pay for a private school, or for them to go to a technical school.

And when the money for fees is not immediately available, weavers are not afraid to take out bank loans. This is how Alphonsine manages education costs.

Weaving gives me a weekly or monthly earning which gives me confidence to go to the bank and to get credit to pay for my children school fees. I repay the loan with the money I get every month.

Théodore Rutagengwa, fifty-five, lives in Byimana sector and is married to a member of the Abahuje weaving cooperative. He has eight children between the ages of twenty-eight and five. He used to work in construction, but due to illness, he is no longer able to practice his profession nor even to cultivate his family's land. It is thanks to his wife's income that two of their children are in high school.

It's my wife who pays for all of their educational expenses. For one child, we pay 25,000 francs each trimester, and 30,000 francs for the other. One studies in Nyanza and the other is in Byumba.

His wife borrows the fees from the other members of her cooperative.

If my wife wasn't weaving, we wouldn't have any children in school or anything at home.

Saving for the Future

Very few rural Rwandese earn enough money to be able to save. This means that they live day to day, without the possibility to put money aside or, as described above, to purchase animals or pay for school fees. Of the weavers, 37.5 percent say they save money and of these, 66.6 percent have opened personal bank accounts since they became weavers. Those who do not have their own accounts engage in communal credit and loan programs through rotating funds (group arrangements in which each person contributes a certain amount, from which one or two persons on a rotating basis take a lump sum as a loan), or within their cooperatives.

The Abahuje craftswomen are particularly well positioned to save. As they sell their baskets weekly, their income is regular and predictable. Local officials, their association leaders, and Gahaya Links all encourage the weavers to save, noted Thérèse.

Janet and Joy [of Gahaya Links] and someone from the Ministry of Commerce came to the association and told us that we should save some of our money. Dukuze also advises us to save.

Each small group of weavers has its own bank account, as does the cooperative as a whole. The treasurer of each group records the payments and savings of their group. Liberata Kayitesi lives in Mpanda, Byimana, and has been the overall treasurer of the Abahuje cooperative for the past three years. She supervises the treasurers of each of the twenty groups of weavers who form Abahuje, and coordinates their activities. The group and cooperative accounts have built up assets through membership fees and the personal savings of the members.

Most weavers make contributions to the group account as a way to save. For those like Espérance, who do not feel ready to manage an individual account, this is a good method of putting small amounts of money aside.

I save 200 francs a week. I'm not thinking of opening my own account because I don't have much money.

The weavers have established a system for disbursing credit, and use the funds in the cooperative and group accounts to offer loans to group members. Liberata outlined the process through which a woman can receive a loan.

Someone who needs credit can write a letter to the committee of her group. The committee checks and approves it. If they think that it is okay, they pass it to the cooperative committee. The cooperative committee decides whether to provide the woman with the credit or not. Because we don't have a lot of money, the maximum credit that we can give is for 30,000 francs. Most of the credit goes towards school fees, for someone who's in the hospital, or for a death in the family. We don't give loans for income-generating projects or businesses.

Liberata went on to clarify that the cooperative does not ask for a guarantee and that the interest rate is 10 percent per month.

It is for the woman to say how she is going to reimburse the money. If she can pay back in a lump sum, this is fine. If not, the group can deduct money from each basket that she sells. For example, the group can take 500 francs from each basket she sells for 3,000 francs.

The *Union des Banques Populaires du Rwanda*, a national federation of credit unions with branches across the country, puts basic financial services within reach of rural Rwandese. Weavers wanting personal accounts generally turn to one of these credit unions. Thérèse saves some money in the Abahuje cooperative account, but also has her own account at the local Banque Populaire. She also obtained a cooperative loan of 30,000 francs.

It was to pay for my children's school fees. I was sick and wasn't weaving a lot at that time. I paid the money back, with 3,000 francs in interest.

Séraphine shares a Banque Populaire account with her husband.

We opened the account in 2006. It was my own idea to open the bank account. When I came here, I exchanged ideas with the other women and decided that I should save. The local authorities also advised us to save, and even the President talks about the value of saving.

Stephanie has an account separate from that of her spouse. In saving, their children are forefront in their minds.

My account is intended for the use of my nine year-old son, and my husband's account is intended for our daughter.

Master weavers like Aristude, president of the Abahuje group in Kibanda cellule, have particular opportunities to accrue capital. Gahaya Links employs them periodically to teach in one- or two-week long weaving courses at their training center in Kigali, and pays them lump sums larger than many have ever held in their hands at once. Before joining Abahuje, Aristude "never had enough money to save anything," but then last year she had the chance to serve as a weaving instructor.

When I opened the account, I had 75,000 francs that I had saved. I got this money after teaching in a weaving workshop. I was paid more than this, but I spent some and then put the rest into the account. At my home, we are poor, but not that poor. It was a surprise for me to get all of this money and so I immediately decided to open an account. I learned some things about saving from the radio, but it was really my own initiative to open the account. I plan on continuing to save more money in the bank as a basis for going into business when I can no longer weave.

Under Rwandese development policies, borrowing, saving, and investing are seen as keys to overcoming poverty. There are a growing number of credit and savings cooperatives and micro-finance agencies across the country that provide further options for weavers to manage their money. Séraphine Nyirafurere is president of a credit and savings cooperative in the Byimana area called Abiteganyiriza, which now has six hundred and one members, many of whom are weavers. She discussed how the loan system there was established and what women use it for.

The women wanted the money they were earning from weaving to be useful and to be able to take out credits. So now, for example, if a woman needs materials, she can come to the cooperative to get credit, or to pay school fees, or to buy animals and improve their agricultural activities.

While the peace basket weavers have not reached the same level of stability as those weaving for Abahuje, Dévota says that she makes efforts to save.

I'm able to save some money for family emergencies. Weaving is something extraordinary if there is a market that's regular. If the market was steady and we had confidence in it, I could save.

Emmanuel Musengimana told of a system for saving among the members of the Ubumwe cooperative.

Each month every person pays 200 francs. It was a way of teaching us the culture [of saving]. This money helps us to buy materials for weaving before we receive money for baskets, and it also goes towards buying books of record for the Association. We also use it to make contributions to people; for example, we recently gave 1000 francs each to two girls who got married. Members can also borrow without paying interest.

The economic power and freedom gained by women weavers have had profound consequences for themselves, their families, and their communities.

CHAPTER 4

Altering Marital Relationships

It would be no exaggeration to say that profitable employment as basket weavers is revolutionizing the way in which weavers and their husbands coexist. The shifts in power, decision-making, and gender roles represent a significant move away from what would be considered traditional marital norms in Rwanda, characterized by a patriarchal structure. Financial stability is easing the strains of poverty on weavers' families, leaving space for calm to enter their homes. Whereas many husbands formerly struggled to fulfill their roles as the sole breadwinner in the family, women weavers, regardless of their age, are able to provide for themselves and also contribute to their families' sustenance. The improvements in their quality of life, as a result of basket sales, have prompted many men to value and admire their wives. Their increased respect in turn fosters a willingness to hold candid discussion and dialogue with their wives; many women say they now decide alongside their husbands how to direct family resources.

But the majority of female basket weavers are still a very long way from rejecting the traditions and beliefs that oppress women, which are deeply ingrained in their families, communities, and in ways that they themselves think and lead their own lives. Although basket weaving has brought harmony in some households, in others it has introduced tension.

It will take a long time for women in rural Rwanda to take permanent and comfortable positions next to their husbands as equals, a process that will be influenced not only by employment possibilities but also by national developments that touch on education, legal reform, political changes, and a host of other factors. The path will be long and difficult, but the progress and optimism that many basket weavers demonstrate is an encouraging platform from which to build a more hopeful future.

Easing the Stresses of Desperation and Dependence

"When people are sharing a few things, they call each other thieves." Immaculée Muhimpundu, the executive of Nyakabuye cellule in Gitarama, drew on this Rwandese proverb to express her thoughts on how poverty creates friction that financial stability and increased wealth help alleviate. Françoise Ntakirutimana, who also heads a cellule where there are many weavers, has observed this same dynamic at play.

> *When a family has food, drink, and money, they live together in harmony. This isn't the case when they are poor.*

In Rwanda, fathers and husbands are expected to take sole or primary responsibility for looking after their wives and children. Evariste Mpayimana argued that for men whose wives do not weave, the pressure to fulfill this role is hard to bear, particularly when they find themselves unable to provide everything their families need.

> *In families without weavers, the man is responsible for the house and the family. Men don't have many jobs that can help them earn a decent income,*

and there isn't enough land for everyone. If men don't have enough money to buy food or take care of things at home, there are bound to be quarrels. It's not easy for men to buy clothes, so if your wife asks for kitenge *and you don't respond, this can also lead to an argument.*

The strain and discontent that build up as a result of such exchanges are why, Evariste says, "Marriages often turn sour because of hunger and poverty."

Catherine Bwinturo illustrates how she feels "relationships between husbands and wives have improved," using the example of a woman who weaves and earns 3,000 francs every week.

If she's making that much, she can buy salt and clothes and this reduces tensions caused by poverty. When a woman isn't making any money, she has to ask her husband for money. And if the husband doesn't have it, then an argument might erupt. But now, such conflicts are becoming less common.

Rather than turning to her husband for what she needs, which sometimes resulted in "tension or confusion," Yvette says she cannot fully express the relief she feels knowing that she can now buy things herself. The fact that weavers contribute to the upkeep of their homes and children helps them and their partners avoid the resentment created by total dependency and the general unease that results from want.

Celine Wambajimana, the head of her weaving group in Ruhashya, said that as a consequence of weaving she now sees less begging around the sector office.

Many parents used to come and ask for assistance in paying school fees. Weaving also has helped people to purchase better clothing. There are orphans who are heads of households who now weave and, through the money they get, they can feed their siblings.

Every member of our cooperative can pay for healthcare coverage. You can't find a family amongst us where the children and the family members don't have enough to eat. But among other families, you can easily encounter all of these problems.

A Sense of Independence

Indeed, a feeling of independence emerges through crafting baskets for sale. The worry that they are a burden on their husbands, or parents, and communities, is a source of frustration, embarrassment, and shame that weavers are glad to have escaped. By helping to assure their families' futures, female artisans sense that, rather than solely relying on others, they are now contributors in their own right.

Séraphine Mukarubwera is happy that her ability to purchase needed items no longer hinges on whether her husband can bring money home and give it to her.

> *I can now make a plan about how to spend the money I earn, and buy whatever I need. I no longer have to wait to see if my husband will give me money. I used to worry that my husband wouldn't buy me new clothes. Now, I just buy them myself.*

A few years ago, before Joseline Kanyange learned how to make baskets, she was living with her parents.

> *I relied on my parents for everything like clothes, shoes, hair cream, washing soap, and other things. It was obviously a strain for them. With weaving, I can afford to look after myself and to supplement my parents' income.*

Now married and living in her own home, Joseline finds that weaving has kept her from depending on her husband and that she no longer has to borrow money or purchase thing on credit as she did before.

Husbands like François Ntambara are pleased to have partners with whom they share financial responsibility.

> *The traditional culture of men earning household income on their own is left only in a few places. These days we say that women are also capable. I'm fine with this. Because now your wife can earn money and you can use this when you are broke.*

When young single women have attained a level of self-sufficiency, it is clear that they will not be wives who look to their husbands to meet their every need. Tharcisse Kaberuka spoke with fatherly pride of the role he knows his daughter will play in her future home.

I'm happy when I see young girls who can now pay to have their hair braided, or to buy oil. When I see that my daughter is capable of supporting herself, I know that when she marries, her wedding won't be a burden to me because she will be able to contribute. And I know that when she has her own home, she will be able to help participate in its management.

What has liberated Angélique Dusabe, above all else, is the knowledge that she is no longer "a recipient." She is not married and lives with her mother and father in Gatovu, Ruhashya. Despite a disability that makes it hard for her to do physical work, she is able to see to her upkeep as she feels a young woman of twenty-two should.

As a disabled person, it wasn't possible for me to till the land to ensure our survival, so I had to rely totally on my parents and the community in my village. But now I'm an independent person. Instead of waiting to receive, I give to others.

Even more painful than relying on a husband working hard to look after his family, is life as a widow. In Rwanda, the death of a woman's husband often puts her fate in the hands of her in-laws and her own parents. She can only hope for their good will and generosity to assure that she and her children have a place to live and a means of survival. As a result of the 1994 genocide, and also due to HIV/AIDS, illnesses, and accidents, widowhood in Rwanda is a common condition. With high birth rates, widows are often left to fend not only for themselves but also for as many as four, five, or six children.

When he compares the situation of widows in the past to today, Théodore Rutagengwa, can see the positive impact of women's employment.

When I was young, a widow would go back to her parents' home, with her children, because she wasn't able to care for them on her own. But now, if the husband dies, the woman can take care of her children. She has different ways of making an income and being responsible for herself and for her children.

Profits from selling baskets allow Consolée Mukaremera and other widows like her to breathe more easily.

If I didn't have this money, my children would be wandering all over the place. But as things are, they stay at home and are happy. They have hope and faith. Widows are often scorned because they have nothing and are forced to beg. But now that I work, I can have pride in myself and my family and feel that my community respects me. I can see to the education and future of my children.

Another widow, Alphonsine Mukamugema, treasures her ability to be financially independent.

Because of the money I get from weaving, I don't need relatives to come to my rescue or care for my family. I used to be totally dependent on people's generosity and was always begging for food, clothes and salt.... But now, I'm not a beggar anymore. I can pay my children's school fees, they don't miss meals as they used to, and I can even lend money to my needy friends.

Gaining in Respect and Equality

As a weaver begins to earn an income that is often greater than her husband's, the respect that he has for her grows. Sharing the task of putting food on the family's table gives him respite and eases her sense of helplessness and vulnerability. Husbands appreciate their wives' participation in raising their families' standard of living; they can see the tangible benefits of their wife's work. These factors, resulting from weavers' gainful employment, are changing how many couples relate to each other by fostering a greater sense of partnership, collaboration, and accord.

"My husband doesn't think of me as a burden anymore," said Stephanie Yankurije, "now that I don't come to him with every small thing." This change in the way he looks at her represents a significant step towards forging a strong and equal relationship with her spouse.

Séraphine has worked hard for her family.

My husband had to see to everything, but he wasn't making good money. I'm the one who's helping the family a lot these days. My husband sees that I'm responsible and that I can accomplish anything. When we got married, we were living in small house. We've expanded it and I have plans to cement the house. My husband is delighted because I'm helping us invest in a better future.

Catherine has observed that when women travel to Kigali to train others, they return with hard-earned wages that inspire the esteem of their partners.

When the woman comes home, she becomes like a guest, and so the husband has to respect her. Traditionally, it was men who would go away and work for money, and when they came back, the women would also honor and respect them. Now, the difference is that the women are going out rather than the men.

Recognizing her financial worth to the family, Rosalie Nakabonye's husband treats her with greater deference.

Because I bring in money, he no longer harasses me as he used to. He knows that I have value in our family. My children are all still young, but I know that they will also respect me because I'm the one who contributes the most towards their survival.

When Josephine Mukantembe attracts praise due to the benefits of weaving, this also reflects well on her husband.

I used to ask my husband for money to buy things. He would get upset and ask what the money was for. Nowadays, I can buy fabric for myself and people say, "That's the wife of So-and-So, and she looks nice and is clean." This pleases my husband.

When a woman spends her day weaving to earn money, she will be more determined to influence how family resources are spent; when a husband respects his wife, he is more apt to listen to what she has to say. Many craftswomen, therefore, report that the way in which decisions are made in their homes is evolving. Husbands hear out their wives' opinions and they discuss family matters side-by-side before settling on the best course.

Godelieve Mukagatera in Kinkanga said that she and her husband "have long conversations before reaching decisions about what is best for the family."

My husband is supportive of my work because it's making it possible for us to care for the children and especially to pay the school fees for the three in high school. My husband is aware of the situation here and of what I do. Everyone knows the price of each basket and my husband knows how many baskets I make, so there aren't any secrets. Weaving doesn't cause any conflicts between us. The only hitch is when there is no market. Then my husband wonders why there is no money coming from my activities.

Rosalie explained why she now has more influence over how her home is run.

Decision-making in our family has changed. I used to be at the receiving end because I wasn't making any contributions to the household income. But today, I bring in a big portion of it, and so I have a say in how decisions are taken in the family.

As 24,000 francs of her family's monthly expenditures rely on her earnings, Godansi Mukabahizi's husband asks for her thoughts on household purchases.

I never used to have a say, even on small matters such as buying things for the house. I just used to watch my husband buying what he thought was a good idea. He would never think to discuss with me what do with the money or ask for my ideas about how we could progress. He despised my ideas. This is no longer the case. Today he asks me what I think he should buy for us. He no longer looks down on my ideas.

Although Séraphine spends long hours weaving, she feels that the money from every basket belongs to her family, and is not hers alone.

When I get money, I bring it home and tell my husband that I have this amount of money. And then we discuss together how we'll spend it. In Rwandese society, when you buy an animal for example, people see it as something that belongs to the family, and not just to the husband or the wife. We don't say this is for me and this is for you. We agree together on what we purchase and we share everything.

Espérance Mukanyandwi sees things slightly differently. She believes that she should in fact have not only equal but greater power in determining where her earnings are spent, as they are the fruits of her personal labor.

My husband and I control the money in the house together. The money is used to pay for things we need. After getting the money, I go home and show it to my husband and explain to him what we need and then I go and buy those things. I take more responsibility over things in our home. I'm the one who gets the money, so I'm able to determine what to do with it, but I inform my husband.

Respect and a sense of partnership between spouses not only lead to discussions of family finances but also promote dialogue about other subjects. Having worked as a weaver and a basket entrepreneur for the last fifty years, Catherine Bwinturo is in a strong position to reflect on how marital relations between weavers have evolved. She sees that a greater sense of equality between partners has improved their ability to listen to one another and to reach compromise, crucial skills to maintaining a stable relationship.

Traditionally, if women fell out with their husbands, they would move back home to their parents' house. But now they are equals and can sit down and mull over things together. It's no longer possible for women to just leave their homes and return to their parents. It was ignorance and lack of education that led them to abandon their homes; they didn't think that it was possible for them to sit down, talk with their husbands and find a solution.

She believes that the change has also promoted a greater sense of camaraderie and that couples spend more time together.

These days, weavers and their husbands can work together, go to church together, and go to the bar together.

Couples in which both husband and wife are weavers "truly become partners," commented Françoise Ntakirutimana.

One of them will weave the top of the basket and the other the bottom. They both understand the benefits of weaving and they work together to finish the basket quickly. They sit side by side while they weave, and so they talk about everything.

Cyprien Bayingana weaves with his wife and compared their relationship prior to his imprisonment and now that they share the same profession.

Before I went to jail, I didn't spend much time at home. I was a businessman and used to sell alcohol. I didn't sit and discuss things with my family; I'd go directly from the field to the bar. But now I don't drink, and we spend the whole day together. I've changed. Now we get along well, talk about everything, and advise each other.

They begin the day working in the fields, and then sit down with their papyrus, sisal, and banana fibers to make peace baskets.

Families of weavers are especially close because when they are weaving, they talk together. When the husband is making the top and the wife the bottom, they are working towards the same goal. They plan together what to do with the money. Even if they're drinking, they can share the beer together.

The time spent together, he is convinced, reinforces their mutual understanding.

People who go their separate ways in the morning are likely to question each other about how much they've earned, what they were doing, and who they were with. And it's also different when the husband doesn't weave. If a woman makes a basket that's rejected, and she goes a long time without earning money, her husband might not understand why. He'll ask his wife why she isn't farming and tell her that she's useless.

Shifting Gender Roles

Women who spend their days weaving, often away from home, must have someone else care for their children, cook, and watch over their homes. Only a few of the weavers can afford to hire domestic workers, so their husbands have to step in and perform the tasks generally reserved for women. While some, realizing the importance of their wives' work, take on these duties willingly, others do so reluctantly.

In Vestine Mukeshimana's view, government policies are critical factors in helping men understand the changing reality in Rwanda.

At the level of the government, people are saying that you have to let women work to make money and develop themselves. So my husband can't tell me to stay at home. He knows that there isn't anything else for me to do. He respects the fact that women have to be more active.

As a local leader, Immaculée knows most of the families in her cellule and the challenges that they confront. She is familiar with their marital dynamics and observed that "weaving improves gender relations."

Before the women started weaving, they never could have imagined that their husbands could cultivate, plant, care for the children, and cook. But now, their husbands are doing all of these things because they see that their wives are working for the good of the home. So the wife can say, "I won't be home today because I've been invited to a workshop." And her husband will respond, "Okay, you should go."

Théodore is one husband who willingly takes over his wife's household chores. He is no longer able to work himself because of illness, and was firm in saying he does not mind looking after his children while his wife weaves. "There is nothing else I can do."

This means that I'm doing woman's work, but I feel good about it. If my wife couldn't weave, we would have nothing at home as I can't make any money. I feel lucky that my wife is earning an income. It's a good arrangement. We are partners at home and we complement each other.

Thérèse Mukangarambe also found this new form of complementarity in her home.

My husband knows that I come here to make money, and so when our oldest child is away at school, he can stay home cooking and taking care of the other children. Sometimes he cooks when I'm busy trying to finish an order. I can't say that he likes to do this, but he doesn't have a choice. I hope to have a house girl in the future, but for the moment, I don't have one.

Pascasie Mukaburigo told of a husband and wife who weave together in the Kinkanga Dufatanye weaving group.

In the evening, the husband leaves first and goes home with the children. He prepares the house and cooks before his wife returns home. Their occupation is reversing their family roles.

That his wife should weave while he stayed home was a mutual decision that Evarsite and Séraphine came to after reflecting on the fact that she can earn more.

Cooking isn't difficult for me. To take the sweet potatoes from their field isn't hard. We are committed to each other. My wife makes the money; I wear good shoes, shirts, and pants.

He added that other weavers and their spouses share work in the same way. He gestured toward the twenty women gathered to work on their baskets.

They have been here since the morning. They have children. You can assume that the husbands are taking care of their children. Any man who recognizes the benefits of weaving can't keep his wife away from work.

Besides assisting with domestic chores, Evariste also tries to facilitate his wife's weaving.

I help them by going to Kirengeri to fetch their materials. Besides carrying the materials, I also know how to weave. If my wife is away or sick, I can monitor the women's weaving. I don't weave regularly, but I know how to. This morning, I gave the women a hand dyeing their raffia because I saw that they might not have enough.

Other men help their wives in similar ways, commented Catherine.

For example, if a woman doesn't have sisal, her husband can wake up early to go and look for some.

Potential Sources of Conflict

Overall, weavers say, the impact of weaving on marital relationships has been positive. Some couples have adapted to the shifts in power balance and in decision-making more easily than others. Changes in the status quo cannot occur overnight and without some friction. Some men are attached to how things were in the past, and are unwilling to tolerate (let alone embrace) changes in traditional gender roles. Some feel diminished or affronted when they see their wives become independent and confident, leaving home regularly to work, and controlling their own money. Even if such men represent a minority, as reflected in the interviews, it is important to recognize that the consequences of gainful employment are sometimes themselves the trigger for anger and resentment, and even violence.

One of the most common sources of discord is who determines how money is spent. Vestine Mukandikwe feels free to spend her money as she wants, "but not all families are the same."

There are some women here who have to go and give their earnings directly to their husbands. And the husband controls the money even though it's the woman who earned it. It isn't good that you spend your time making money, and then your husband can say, "Give me the money." This isn't fair because you're the one who worked for it. Among my group of fifty here, there aren't many women whose husbands behave like this, but it's not uncommon in some of the other groups.

Although Espérance's husband does not demand complete control over her earnings, he is reluctant to let her spend it without his approval, especially when he wants a drink.

When we agree that we're going to spend money on things, things go okay. But one day I came here to get money. I bought many things and had no money when I reached the house. My husband said to me, "You didn't even save some money for me to drink with? The money here is for one bottle, this isn't enough for me to drink with." He was angry, but we made up quickly. This doesn't happen often. But if he's been drinking and sees that I haven't finished making lunch, he sometimes lashes out.

Because she is president of the women's council in her cellule, many come to Thérèse when there are misunderstandings. She offered an example:

A man may ask his wife to give him money for beer. But she's reluctant because she knows there are more important things to do with the money. This can result in an argument, and sometimes the woman will call me to come to her home to mediate and find a way to stay together peacefully. But situations like this aren't as common anymore.

Evariste explained that men also are sometimes unwilling to shoulder domestic chores, which can cause friction.

While some husbands are ready to cook and to gather the bananas because their wives are weaving, some don't want their wives to weave. And even those who stay at home and cook can be heard to complain about it. I advise them to let their wives be free and earn money.

It is not always easy for a husband to assume responsibilities that he has grown up seeing as women's work, as Espérance pointed out.

It would be great if the husband could do everything that his wife does at home. That is today's challenge. Women are weaving and also seeing to things at home. Some husbands help in the house and are good at what they do. But when you leave him to do this everyday, he might end up telling you that it's not his responsibility.

A Shield Against Domestic Violence?

It is difficult, in general, for women and men to discuss openly a subject as sensitive as violence against women, and even more so when there is an aggressive government campaign to discourage it. Previous research by African Rights on violence against women in Rwanda (see *Women Taking a Lead: Progress Towards Empowerment and Gender Equity in Rwanda*, October 2004) found that much of the violence women endure is inflicted by members of their extended family, making discussion even more taboo. Physical and psychological abuse, even when it is of an extreme nature and committed against a minor, and even if it amounts to incest, is considered a private matter to be settled within the family. To accuse a husband, a brother-in-law, or cousin is tantamount to betrayal of the family and will be discouraged vigorously, including by women themselves, seemingly out of concern for the reputation of the family or even the victim herself whose marriage prospects may be at stake. In rural Rwanda, as in any other poor country, it would take enormous and unusual courage for an uneducated woman with few skills to defy her family and, in the case of a married woman, her in-laws, by denouncing a close relative against the advice of the family that is her only form of economic and social security. For all these reasons, women remain silent and secretive about abuses within the family. African Rights approached a number of weavers to talk specifically about the issue of domestic violence. Despite an initial reluctance, they eventually opened up and made a number of revealing statements.

Although weaving seems to be having an overall positive impact, domestic abuse still occurs in the lives of some families. Sometimes, change itself is the trigger for violence, as men use the disruption as a new excuse to turn against their wives.

The Isangano association was established in 2002 in the town of Gitarama to address the problems of rural women, and included both weavers and non-weavers. In a group discussion with many members, there was general consensus that in their region domestic violence "runs riot," to use the words of one woman. Asked how weavers fared, they gave a mixed response.

Having in place a basket weaving project has changed very little in the family life of those women who partake in the project. It's true that they have more money to improve their economic situation, but in certain families it is actually a source of argument and domestic violence instead of being a solution. However, in other families the employment has had a very positive impact and domestic violence is no longer on the same level as before.

Thérèse, a member of Isangano who runs a restaurant, had this to say:

Through the basket weaving or other associations, women receive counsel from each other and learn how to look after themselves. Some men have changed their attitudes towards their wives since they have started to bring money into the house. However, for other men, it has become a source of resentment and they don't want their wives to go out and earn money. Frequently, there are households that give the impression that there is no domestic violence, but sexual violence is very common and often stays just between the man and the woman.

Men like Cyprien believe that a greater focus on family economics among weavers has reduced overt violence.

There is less aggression than before. Violence was mostly caused by the hard liquor we used to drink, which isn't so popular now. People have to put their heads together to make a living and that's why families are getting to know each other and live together better.

An official in her cellule, Françoise Ntakirutimana said she had not received reports of domestic violence "for a long time."

If you beat your wife, you'll be arrested. Yes, domestic violence can occur. But there are specific cases, rather than a widespread general problem.

Evariste, who blames alcohol for much of the violence against women, says that fear of punishment is a deterrent.

Some men who drink a lot may also beat their wives, but not often. There are no secrets about this. If you try to beat your wife because you had to cook and care for the children, your wife can go to the local authorities and you'll go straight to jail.

Catherine says that it used to take little for a man to beat his wife, saying even simple problems commonly led to quarrels and bruises. She blames "poverty and ignorance," but also the fact that women themselves had too much time on their hands.

Before, women had enough time to gossip and spread rumors with other women. This sometimes caused conflicts between husbands and wives. For example, a woman could talk to her neighbor about an argument that she's had with her husband. Perhaps the neighbor will tell someone else, and eventually it will get back to the woman's husband and he'll beat her for talking about him. But now, everyone is busy with her own activities. Women are weaving and selling baskets and don't have time to talk about these things. Women are appreciated more than they were in the past and this is also why men don't beat them.

Eugenie Nyanzira, a widow who teaches other women to weave in the Byimana sector, is also convinced that physical assaults in her area have greatly diminished because "women are more valued."

There are only a few cases. There were men in the rural areas who beat their wives. They looked upon them as useless as they didn't bring in any money. And so violence was sometimes provoked by women's very dependence on their husbands. They'd make demands, and the husbands would respond with aggression.

Eugenie also attributes the reduction in assaults to the fact that violence against women has now become a matter of public debate.

Training about women's rights and gender has become common. And because the government has resolved to speak about this publicly, even in these local training sessions and meetings we can talk about domestic violence against women openly, so that everyone knows and is conscious of the stance that he or she should take. The Réseau de Femmes in Gitarama, which has branches in rural areas, is behind some of the training.

Weaving in particular "has played a role in preventing violence against women," according to Judith.

Poverty, or the fact that a woman has nothing to do, can have a lot to do with violence. A young woman who lives near Gitarama and has no job can go into town and spend the night there. Men may well target her because they see that she's just wandering around. But weavers respect themselves. They just weave and then go home to take care of things at home.

In a house where there is poverty, the woman and the man can often go out and come home drunk. If the woman comes home drunk, the husband might beat her. And if the man has no job, he can home late and drunk, because there's nothing at home. This all causes disputes that can result in violence.

Poverty increases disputes in families because if a wife asks for something that her husband doesn't have or can't provide, he might beat her in response. But weaving as an income-generating activity can bring peace between a husband and his wife. They discuss [matters] as equals because the husband sees the importance of his wife. She brings money into the house and so they can speak on the same level.

Although Josephine does not think that beating women is common where she lives, she advised women to "manage well" their newfound economic strength to minimize disagreements at home.

Having money can make you feel that you have more power, and the man feels like you don't respect him, leading to clashes.

Weavers and their spouses, of course, do not live in isolation, with their lives determined solely by the demands and benefits of weaving. Even if there is more food on the table, there might still be arguments about money spent on alcohol, said Evariste.

Even men who are working and making money spend some money on drinks before they reach home. When they return, their wives will say to them, "You waste money drinking when there isn't food in the house and when we need clothes?" And if the man is drunk, they can start to fight and he can beat her.

Infidelity, as Stephanie underlined, also brings violence into the home.

Some of the women have husbands who beat them. If you suspect that he's been with another woman, or with a prostitute, you can't accept this and you no longer get along with your husband. And then he might strike you because of this.

Drocella (a pseudonym) in Ruhashya said she felt constrained to hand over her earnings to her husband "so that my children and I can have peace in our home."

He always knows exactly when I will be paid and how much. And he starts demanding that I hand over the money as soon as I arrive home, to buy beer, cigarettes, to pay the laborers. If I don't do so, he starts a fight.

Asked what she thought about his behavior, Drocella's response highlighted the discrepancy between the reality in the villages and the discourse on women's rights disseminated by the government and embraced by civil society.

You people from the towns are always talking about gender. But you are only creating difficulties for us. If a woman behaves as if she is emancipated, she is only inviting violence in her home. And she has no one to come to her rescue because even her own parents and siblings are against her.

In this context, she described the money she earns from weaving as a partial shield against violence because it enabled her, she said, "to buy a semblance of peace at home."

When our husbands want to have a go at their wives and children, we weavers have the resources to calm them down and to negotiate. But the village women who don't weave and therefore don't have money get beaten. So our money helps to diminish domestic violence.

Drocella said that she takes advantage of the times her husband is in a good mood to ask for money to buy items like clothes. And she was also careful to protect herself and her children by other means.

Most of us hide one basket we've sold from our husbands, and use the money from that. If he discovered the truth, he could kill me! So I do my best to make sure that he doesn't find out.

Prisca (a pseudonym) in Ruhashya explained the different reactions men had to their wives' new economic positions.

There are forty-five women in our association and at least eighteen of them continue to suffer violence at the hands of their husbands. Some men take a positive attitude and see the money their wives earn as a contribution to the family's finances. But some want their wives to remain housewives, arguing that a woman who makes her own money will not obey her husband. As a result, they force their wives to stop weaving. They don't allow them to work, and treat them like children.

Prisca herself is among the eighteen women she cited.

I myself was beaten three times by my husband because of the money from basket weaving. The first time, it was two months after he was released from prison. I had just sold baskets for 24,000 francs, but after paying off what I owed, I was left with 14,000. He demanded that I give him all the money and became furious when he saw that it was less than the total value of the baskets. The second time, he forbade me from going to the association. I insisted and he damaged the basket. I went anyway, without his permission. He was like a lion when I came home, and pounced on me, beating me black and blue until my neighbors became concerned and saved my life.

The third time, it was really catastrophic. He was standing next to me when I was paid, and demanded the money as reimbursement for the food I ate while he was in prison. We argued, and he grabbed the money by force and then turned on me. Again, neighbors came to my rescue. I can't leave him, unless I see that he really does intend to kill me, because I have nowhere to take my four children.

Women who feel isolated and lonely, and who are cut off from the support networks that emerge out of shared endeavors and professional associations, will have even less protection against violence. They will have fewer opportunities to learn new skills, will be less open to new developments, and will be less informed about what is happening in their region and in the country as a whole. The importance not only of weaving, but of the connections made between women as they weave, remains central to the issue of domestic violence. In many settings the associations provide countless women with a new, safer, and enlarged extended family.

CHAPTER 5

Others To Lean On

RELATIONSHIPS AMONG WEAVERS

As members of associations and cooperatives, weavers are drawn out of their homes to sit and work with their fellow artisans several times a week. Collaboration through work forges close bonds of trust and friendship. There are more women who can visit them when they are sick or lend them money when the need arises. Wherever they spread grass mats and lay down their raw materials and tools, becomes their work area, and they gather not only for work but also for discussion: they ask questions and share emotional and practical problems. Being with others has opened up the weavers' minds to new ideas, which together with their new economic reality has made them more optimistic about the future.

Although weavers are all poor and rural, there are many differences between them, and being together promotes their openness and acceptance of each other. The groups include genocide survivors but also wives, daughters, and sisters of imprisoned perpetrators and genocide suspects, as well as convicted killers themselves, all participating together in single associations of weavers. The fact that they join together, and side by side stitch and intertwine natural fibers, forces them to interact, whereas they would otherwise maintain separate and distinct social circles and avoid approaching each other. Weaving, therefore, has a definite constructive impact on reconciliation in that it brings people together. However, the wounds caused by the 1994 genocide and the fault lines it drew throughout communities are deep, so deep that there are certain points which shared labor and regular interaction have not been able to touch, let alone bridge. So there are persistent tensions within communities where women and men are learning to work together.

Emerging from Isolation

For a rural Rwandese wife or mother, daily life centers around cultivating the soil around her dwelling, tending to her animals, preparing meals, and caring for her children. Homes in Rwanda are sprinkled over the hills of the countryside, separated by fields of crops and banana trees. Therefore, regular contact and exchanges with people outside of the immediate family unit are limited, with the exceptions of going to the market, to church, or attending *gacaca* trials. Thérèse Mukarugwiza's description of her daily routine prior to weaving reflects that of many other women.

> *I would wake up and spend the day cultivating, without meeting or interacting with other people. I was alone and quiet. But now I'm a member of this group.*

Living in Ruhashya, Godansi Mukabahizi rarely ventured far from her *umudugudu* in Gitwa.

> *My daily life, as a housewife, revolved around tending to my gardens, working in the kitchen, fetching water and firewood, and things like that. I never had time to join community meetings or women's groups or to visit other women.*

Spending entire days sitting and working for hours alongside their neighbors has led weavers to maintain an unprecedented level of interaction with those living in their area. All of them welcome this change. During the seasons when they are not planting or harvesting, rural women find themselves with free time and not very much to do. In Buheshi, Ruhashya, Françoise Mukamana has observed that keeping busy through basket-making helps social harmony.

When people don't have an occupation and are idle, they are more likely to create conflict and get into arguments with others. But with weaving, we are always occupied. We don't have time to wander around and make trouble.

Théodore Rutagengwa agrees with this assessment and is glad to see that his wife's work creates cohesion among women.

Before, there were some women who just sat around during the dry season without anything to do. They'd just criticize other people, gossip, and get into disputes with each other. But now, the women come here and are together. They teach each other, share their problems at home, and offer each other suggestions and advice.

School is the primary means through which children are socialized, but when she became eleven, Athanasia Mukayandwi started missing classes to care for her sick mother. For ten years, she spent most days at home with her mother and her sister, who is mentally ill. In May 2006 she joined other weavers in the Ubumwe cooperative.

I used to feel isolated and depressed. But now I'm in contact with many others and I'm more open to my community. When we're in the association together, we meet people who we didn't know before. We talk and form friendships, all in a good atmosphere.

Weavers have found companions among their colleagues. Seeing Alphonsine Mukamugema chat with the other women around her, it's hard to believe her when she says, "Before I joined the weaving association, I didn't know many people."

Through weaving, I've gotten to know other people and made friends, both among weavers and with women who come to learn from me. These friends have helped me in so many ways, for example, by lending me money, giving me advice, and visiting me when I'm sick.

Indeed, the bonds they form extend far beyond baskets and business, commented Consolée Mukaremera.

The weavers here feel a sense of solidarity. We have learned to be honest with each other and have built an atmosphere of trust. As we are friends, when one of the members has a party, we help each other and contribute. Outside of work, we see each other and spend time together and feel free to ask each other for assistance.

Within her group in Kibanda, Aristude Mukashyaka both offers and receives assistance and care.

We all have good relationships with each other. If someone's child is sick, she can't be kept from going to the hospital because of money. You can give her money so that she can go. If there's a girl who's going to get married, we can prepare a gift for her as weavers.

Just a few months after Rose (a pseudonym), who was not married, became a member of the Dukundane association in Rwaniro, she became pregnant. Feeling embarrassed, she retreated back into her home. She spoke of feeling as though people did not want to approach her and so she avoided going out in public and being among the other weavers. But after she gave birth, the men who had first taught her to weave paid her a visit.

They convinced me to come back and weave with the others again. This felt so good. They told me that everything would be fine. Before, I thought that perhaps I'd keep weaving, but just stay at home. I used to feel alone and thought the others wouldn't allow me back into the association again. But they told me there was no problem. They wanted to help me.

With her baby tied to her back, she held a half-finished basket between her knees and said, "Now I feel at home here and relaxed, talking to people and knowing people."

They accepted me and advised me to come and talk things over. Grown-ups talk to us younger weavers. Some of them told me to persevere, saying that having a child isn't the end of the world and that these things can happen.

She has in fact found a greater level of acceptance from her co-weavers than from her own family.

My parents would abuse me, and swear at me, because of my child. But now I spend the day out of the house here, with people who take me for what I am. I get suggestions from my co-workers about how to manage my relationship with my parents. They console me and tell me how to act when my parents are mean to me, telling me that I should go on as normal and be patient.

In addition to the kindness, openness, and goodwill of the other weavers, Rose also points to her new economic stability as helping her connect with others.

When someone is poor, others isolate that person. When you are isolated, you feel lonely and think negative thoughts. But when you have a source of income, people want to know you, to approach you and want to be friends. Socially, we are more co-operative than non-weavers because of [our] daily interaction.

The Dufatanye Genocide Widows' Association in Ruhuha, Bugesera, is new to basket-weaving. Odette Nyirandamutsa, forty-five, has two children who are sixteen and ten. She began weaving one year ago after she heard that there was a demand for baskets, and because she had noticed that weavers "had a good situation, compared to other people." AVEGA found trainers and paid them to work with Bugesera's association which, founded nine years ago, now contains 130 genocide widows from the former commune of Ngenda. Most of these women have lived off agriculture in the past. What Odette most appreciate is "the exchange of ideas with the others."

We are all survivors and some of us felt alone and depressed. Because we meet together on a regular basis, we have formed friendships and feel more hopeful about life. Personally, weaving brought me out of isolation. Talking to the others stops me from constantly dwelling on the effects of the genocide and, as a result, feeling wretched.

Weaving has changed things in the association. Before, we only met for official meetings or gathered together when someone visited and wanted to help us.

Eugenie Mukandanga, who completed five years of primary school, is one of the more experienced weavers in the Dufatanye association and she combines weaving with farming. The mother of one seventeen-year-old child, she sells her baskets to AVEGA. She has used the extra income from weaving, on average about 16,000 francs a month, to hire someone to cultivate her fields, to buy two goats, to cement the floor in her home, and to complete what she proudly described as the "finishing details" in her house. Important as they are, the material purchases are far less significant for her than the emotional advantages of being part of Dufatanye.

Before we began weaving in the association, I felt very much on my own and depressed. Weaving has enabled me to come out of this loneliness. I feel linked to the other members, and useful to them. I feel more a part of my community and more capable of being involved in it. And officials in the sector have been useful in putting us in contact with weaving associations elsewhere in the country, and creating a spirit of connection between us.

I like weaving and I feel proud. Even when I'm at home, to avoid feeling bored or lonely, I weave.

Her optimism has made Eugenie more energetic and confident.

I feel capable of doing other things. I'm president of education in my cellule and I'm vice-president of gacaca in my sector. And there are many others who have dared to take on such roles and participate in governance. Really, it's weaving that motivates us to do this. I feel useful in society and hope to participate in the life of the country.

Talking While Weaving: Advice from All Sides

As weavers busy themselves with their baskets, they keep an eye on the work of their neighbors—to correct, to encourage, and to imitate. They graciously share expertise in weaving, and as hours pass, discussion becomes more personal and moves to their life experiences and challenges. Opening up about the hardships in their lives brings immense psychological relief. Their colleagues do not hesitate to offer advice and guidance and so, together, they talk things through to find solutions.

Françoise Mukamana described how weavers make sure that their weaving companions produce high-quality baskets.

We don't all know how to weave in the same way. There are some who don't know how to make the bottom of the basket, and others who aren't good at finishing the edges. And so we coach each other.

"We also exchange experiences while we weave," added Françoise.

We have all led different lives, and so have different ideas and information to share. One person's knowledge can complement and supplement what someone else has to say. We learn about what's happening in this area and in the country. We talk sometimes about politics, and hear about the latest news. We stay informed.

Having lost two of her own children and now caring for an HIV-positive orphan, Esther sometimes feels like life has dealt her a bad hand. But at least now, she doesn't feel alone.

Before coming here, I often felt lonely and distressed. When we are here, I see how other people are living. I used to think that I was the only one with certain worries, but here I've found women who are dealing with the same, or even worse things. This puts things into perspective and makes me feel better about my life.

"Getting involved in this association," says Anatalia Niwemutima, "has helped me a lot."

I used to keep all my troubles to myself, but today I share them with other weavers. And together, we come up with solutions.

Stephanie Yankurije is happy to be among other craftswomen. "I don't feel on my own when I'm faced with a big problem," she says.

I tell the group to see what they think. And if three women all give me the same advice, I'll have a good idea of what I should do.

When Pascal Munyemana's wife comes home after a day of weaving, she always seems well-informed about current news.

If one weaver hears something on the radio, and the others didn't, she tells them what she heard. So they all know about the information that has been passed through the radio.

Pascal is convinced that looking to each other as role models and for guidance helps the weavers improve themselves.

Conflict with their husbands is one predicament that weavers often present to their colleagues with requests for counsel. Because of shifts weaving has caused in marital relations, by altering the traditional division of labor and gender roles, tensions can rise between couples. When this occurs, a woman's fellow weavers are there to step in, both to keep a woman weaving and to preserve marital peace. Rwanda's gender policies are clear in promoting women's employment, so weaving associations know well that they can flex their group muscle before any reticent husband and the local authorities will be there to back them. Stephanie gave an example.

One woman told us about the troubles she and her husband were having, and that he was against her weaving. He said she didn't respect him because she's making her own money through weaving. We advised her to go to the local authorities. The authorities spoke to the husband and helped him to understand that it's good for his wife to work and be productive. He's now okay. This isn't a widespread problem among husbands, but there are some husbands who still have such ideas.

Séraphine Mukamugema recounted a similar story of how women from her group helped ease friction between a weaver and her spouse.

There is one woman who didn't come today, who had a problem once. We went to Gahaya to deliver baskets and came home late. By the time this woman got home, it was late and dark. Her husband refused to open the door for her. He told her, "Go back where you've come from and where you've been spending all of your time!" The woman had to stay at her family's house. Afterwards, a group of weavers went to see that man. They told him that even if his wife was outside the house, she was with other women and doing important things. The man went to his wife and asked her to forgive him, and then they went back to living together.

This is one example of how, she says, "we exchange ideas about living together peacefully with our families and neighbors."

We influence each other to act appropriately. If there is a conflict, we know how to guide each other on what to do and how to resolve it.

Because men are virtually absent in the groups of the Abahuje cooperative, exclusively women's spaces have been formed, where personal and private issues relating to sexuality come up for discussions. In Thérèse Mukangarambe's group in Buhoro, family planning is one subject about which women have passed on information. These conversations, she says, have helped her "to leave ignorance behind."

Before, I wouldn't dream of telling my husband that I didn't want to have sex. But now I spend time with other women. We talk about many things, and I learned from them that refusing sex wasn't a bad thing. So I decided to tell my husband that we shouldn't have any more children.

If it wasn't for weaving and being in an association, I'd still be farming and having babies. My husband and I made the decision to stop having children and to take care of the ones we had. We went to the hospital together and asked for advice. They gave us different options and we made our choice.

Birth rates in Rwanda are high, and so the fact that Thérèse has seven children is nothing out of the ordinary. But women are increasingly conscious of the hardships that large families face. Chantal (a pseudonym) was happy to learn from her colleagues how she can limit her family to the six children she already has. She related how the topic of birth control is sometimes broached.

For example, one woman can ask another, "Your youngest child is five now and you haven't had any more? How did you manage this?" She can tell you that she went to the doctor and got medication and from her you can also learn how to plan your family, and be encouraged to go the doctor.

Before, when I spent most of my time at home, I thought that using birth control would make you get sick or die. But I met other women who have used the pill or had implants or injections and I saw that they were just fine. So I went to the doctor and decided to start taking the pill.

Contributing to Reconciliation?

Reconciliation in the wake of the 1994 genocide of the minority Tutsis is a complex and extremely sensitive issue, often making it difficult to gauge people's true feelings and fears. Reconciliation is used to describe the knitting-together of the social fabric in the wake of bitter and violent conflicts, but it does not of itself provide a pattern for doing so. Truth, justice, and forgiveness have been common threads in efforts to bring about reconciliation in many countries, but the emphasis upon each of them can vary immensely, depending upon the context and the speaker.

Underpinning these issues are the very real economic and social problems which continue to afflict the majority of Rwandese. Conditions of hardship propelled the genocide, and they can undermine people's capacity for change. In this context, the economic benefits from weaving and beading are necessary in giving people a stake in the country's development. Equally important, they provide a much-needed forum for perpetrators of the genocide, or their close relatives, to meet and interact with genocide survivors, and to have shared interests by working together on a common project.

Etienne (a pseudonym), imprisoned for ten years, was released in July 2006 and lives in Rwaniro, Butare. He accepts that he killed a neighbor.

The mother of the person I killed is a weaver and we work together. Weaving made us spend time together. I asked for forgiveness. The victim's family also invited me to join another small farming cooperative.

The neighbors watch us and learn from us. Someone who sees me working alongside the mother of the man I helped to kill is also more likely to approach someone who is opposed to him.

Judith (a pseudonym) weaves with the Duteraninkunga Kamusenyi group in Byimana sector. One of her neighbors is a survivor who lost his wife in 1994 and who lived alone with his children. At first, each kept his distance from the other.

After the genocide, even though I did not take part, I didn't have a good relationship with them.

It was his daughter's wish to weave that broke the ice, according to Judith.

His daughter wanted to learn how to weave because their family was living in misery. She approached me and I taught her. Gradually, we started to visit each other's families, and now we're good friends.

Judith, who blames survivors for the death of her father immediately after the genocide, is convinced that the communal gatherings around weaving are important stepping stones towards reconciliation.

My family was harmed in August 1994 by vengeance crimes. Survivors killed my father, and so I also had a hard time tolerating survivors. I know other people who felt the same way. But weaving became a basis for reconciliation; we joined together and managed to put conflicts aside. There is lingering tension which prevents some people from taking part in gacaca. But after we began to weave, things started to go more smoothly and we've made real progress, especially since 2000.

Concessa (a pseudonym) in Ruhashya says that weaving "has reduced our suspicions of each other."

It means that survivors, orphans, and prisoners all work together, and have a chance to talk about things that aren't going well within the community. I genuinely think that we've done well in this area within our association. Our solidarity in turn helps gacaca because it makes us more able to ask for forgiveness and ready to reveal the truth about who killed who or looted what.

Christine (a pseudonym), who also lives in Ruhashya, said that even the decision to adopt the name "peace baskets" reflects the yearning for harmony and the desire to heal the divisions in their community.

They are called peace baskets because weaving brought us together after the genocide. There are genocide perpetrators released from prison and survivors working side by side, together with people they didn't know before. There was a huge chasm amongst us, but sharing this activity has brought us closer, and is helping us move towards the path of reconciliation.

Christine is modest about their achievements.

We have not achieved 100 percent reconciliation. There are still some misunderstandings between us. When we are together as an association, some people avoid talking about things related to the genocide. Although the baskets are called peace baskets, there are some genocide suspects who have caused conflict amongst us.

What is important, she underlined, is the fact that there is sufficient will to confront problems collectively.

We, all of us, together, denounce the person in the wrong and try to find a solution, so that this person will change. When we are here at work, we try to think about the future and not about our country's dark history.

If someone who belongs to the association is accused in gacaca, we blame him or her as a group. But when we come back to work, we don't treat that person any differently.

Florence (a pseudonym), a survivor in Ruhashya, is also a *gacaca* judge. She is unequivocal in her opinion that weaving has been productive with regard to reconciliation.

There are people who have forgiven each other, and if they weren't weaving together, they would never have been able to reach this point. For example, there is a man who weaves with his son. He committed genocide, but he asked me to pardon him, and I forgave him. He's even the one who taught me how to weave. Liberated prisoners meet with survivors and this creates a sense of cohabitation. It gives us hope in the possibility of living together. Despite everything that happened, people can form friendships through this shared economic activity and the common desire to earn money.

And the reconciliation here has an effect on gacaca trials as well. If this man was able to ask me for forgiveness, this means that he contributed to gacaca and took it seriously.

The unity that we have created amongst us has a wider effect on others in our area. The members of the association are like delegates for those who haven't developed the same sentiments. For example, take me. I can go to my mom and friends and other survivors and tell them that a prisoner who has been released is here and has changed. This encourages others to feel comfortable with him and approach him. And the former prisoners take a positive message to their families and friends about how we can live together.

Marcelline (a pseudonym), a survivor in Nyakabuye, admits that she did not, at first, want to join her weaving association, where many of the members were either perpetrators of the genocide or the wives of men imprisoned on genocide crimes. She gradually opened up.

Now things are okay. I came to see that it's not these women or their husbands who I'm upset with or who were the cause of the genocide. They appreciate this change in my attitude.

She, in turn, values the fact that they encourage each other to speak the truth about the genocide during trials in the local genocide courts of *gacaca*.

Someone can't pretend that they don't know about something because one of the other members will say, "You know about this, say something."

But for the most part, survivors have not learned from their fellow weavers the information about the genocide that is so vital to their emotional recovery and stability. Cansilde in Butare has tried to find out what happened to her children.

> *When we are weaving, we don't talk about matters related to the genocide. But this doesn't mean that I'm not hurting inside. The genocide perpetrators learn a lot from me, but they won't even show me where they buried my children and who killed them. One man told me that he dumped twelve dead bodies in our toilet, but he doesn't mention who they were and who killed them. I suspect though that one of them is my son. They don't realize that this wounds me because I laugh with them and act like everything is okay. But this man's* gacaca *trial is coming up, and then they will see that I am angry.*

Prisca (a pseudonym), also in Butare, is constantly looking for answers that remain elusive.

> *I'm a widow of the genocide, and it will not be easy for me to reconcile with someone who killed my husband and my children, who doesn't even want to tell me how they were killed and where their bodies were thrown. There are some people in our association who were released from prison because they bribed judges in* gacaca *courts, and I'm sure nothing has changed in their hearts. And reconciliation depends, above all, on people's hearts.*

Asked why she thought these former prisoners had not changed, she referred to the local *gacaca* courts.

> *We attend* gacaca *to learn from those who know what took place. But they never say the truth. They made a kind of plot where they transfer all the terrible crimes to the people who are still in exile, or those who have died. As survivors, we find this shocking. Even if we were in hiding during the genocide, we witnessed terrifying killings which claimed the lives of our children, neighbors, and relatives.*

> *When those who are accused, by the very people who saw them participate in genocide, are stubborn in their denials, then to me they are making fun of the genocide because they are refusing to acknowledge the weight of the crimes*

they committed. It will be hard to achieve reconciliation if they continue to take this same attitude.

Colette (a pseudonym) drew a distinction between work and people's private feelings.

Work leads to a sense of camaraderie, but reconciliation is something else completely because it depends on the heart, and the way people who should reconcile see things. You don't have to be friends to work together. Everyone is in the association for their own interests, and to develop themselves.

But Colette is not ready to give up, believing that the daily interaction and the investment in a common endeavor could pave the way towards better relations, reinforced by appropriate training sessions.

Perhaps then people could bring themselves to seek forgiveness from people they had wronged, out of which meaningful reconciliation could come. However, nothing will really change unless people are willing to acknowledge their role in the genocide. And if people are holding back in gacaca, which I have seen myself, how can I expect them to speak up in our weaving association?

Lucie (a pseudonym) took a long time before she answered questions about reconciliation, and prefaced her comments by saying, "You shouldn't always let others see what you think." She admits that, as a survivor, she finds it difficult to weave alongside many of the men and women in her group.

For the sake of your own interests, you can work with someone who has hurt you. It's certainly hard, but you have to persist and be patient if you have no other choice. There are very few survivors in our association because many of the women couldn't bring themselves to sit down with people who were involved in the death of their parents and children, or even to work with the children of women who say that their husbands, jailed for genocide, have been imprisoned for nothing. That hurts us so much.

She gave an example from her own life.

One time the wife of the man who killed my brother said there was no reason why her husband should find himself behind bars, even though it was a well-known case. This kind of language turns the knife in our hearts and is an obstacle to unity and reconciliation between us as weavers.

Lucie criticized her fellow weavers for not shedding light on what happened to her loved ones in 1994, but hopes that attitudes will change with time and effort.

How can we say that there is reconciliation within the group when people don't want to speak openly about everything linked to the genocide? Many of the weavers know exactly who looted and demolished our houses and who killed our families. But they won't tell us. It is a long and painful process, but through meetings and training, people might act differently. If people don't tell the gacaca *courts everything they know, they are not going to do so in a weaving association.*

Adèle (a pseudonym), who said that her group of fifty women in Nyakabuye did not include any survivors, said that "weaving together helps with unity and reconciliation because women from different places were obliged to sit together and talk." But, she added, "We never talk about the genocide here."

The survival of the Rwandese nation depends upon its ability to move forward from tragedy towards peaceful development. It must seek ways of coming to terms with its past and of creating new structures and relationships upon which it can found the future. The journey will be long. But the fact that weavers and beaders with such different experiences and perspectives continue to work together is an important part of this necessary, and difficult, effort.

CHAPTER 6

HIV/AIDS

SPREADING THE WORD AND GIVING STRENGTH

B y breaking the cycle of women's dependence on men, making it possible for them to become decision-makers in their homes and aware of new ideas and rights, weaving has the potential to help stem the tide of the HIV/AIDS epidemic in Rwanda.

Poverty and despair lead women to have unsafe sex for money or material goods. Weavers, however, do not have to engage in such exchanges. Women who are confident and esteemed by their communities also have a greater ability to negotiate safe sex, to retreat from abusive relationships, and to confront their husbands about infidelity. Within their weaving associations, women are discovering more about HIV. Open discussion is helping to lift the veil of ignorance and encourage women to find out more about these serious issues.

In some settings, the subject of HIV/AIDS remains taboo. Where it is openly discussed, some resist testing or listening to advice from their colleagues. Seropositive members of weavers' communities also still feel the weight of stigma. There is a real need to promote formal education to prevent unnecessary infection.

It is a positive achievement that 59 percent of the weavers interviewed for this book have been tested for HIV/AIDS. Most of these women were tested while pregnant, as is now routine in Rwanda. It is also encouraging that 91 percent of those who have not been tested would like to be. This reveals that the desire for testing and education are unmet, and represents a genuine opportunity to provide services which would be welcomed by the weavers themselves.

Preventing the Spread through Economic Empowerment

In the Rwandese countryside, as across the globe, poverty leaves many girls and women vulnerable to men who offer them money or other desired items in exchange for sexual favors. Where need is real and severe, such propositions can be difficult to refuse. Young women are most likely to fall prey to these advances. Weavers say that their earnings have given them the independence to turn down such offers from men. Besides the fact that they can satisfy their own economic needs, weavers are busy and say they do not even have time to entertain such offers. When female weavers discuss HIV/AIDS, they focus on prostitution and promiscuity, which they identify as the principal means through which women contract HIV. Because economic empowerment takes away the financial incentive to have sex, they conclude that weaving plays a role in lowering women's risk, and ultimately can contribute to reducing the prevalence of HIV/AIDS.

Many women highlighted their observations about the ways in which gainful employment and full-time occupation as professional weavers is connected with preventing the spread of HIV/AIDS among young women. Desperation feeds acts of prostitution, said Josephine Mukantembe.

Sometimes people prostitute themselves because they need things. Any man can come and show you money, and then ask for sex, and you end up agreeing.

But when you have money to support yourself, you don't need to be involved in these kinds of things.

Idleness also puts people at risk of infection, according to Françoise Mukamana.

What causes AIDS in this country is that there are people who don't have anything to do and who just hang around bars and wander aimlessly. They might accept money in exchange for sex. And because they don't interact with people who are knowledgeable and aren't involved in the community, they don't get information about AIDS.

But weavers are different, she said, because they have a profession and daily work.

We have an occupation, we feel busy and we are economically independent. Because we exchange ideas amongst us, we learn about things like AIDS and feel informed, involved and a part of the community. I've noticed that most of the people who get AIDS are poor.

Françoise Ntakirutimana concluded by saying that "poverty reduction is one of the most important ways to prevent AIDS." Séraphine Mukarubwera agreed.

A young girl who isn't weaving might say to herself, "I'll have sex with him so I can get nice lotion or dresses." Through weaving, young women can make their own money, so she doesn't have to run the risk of getting HIV just because she wants clothes or some beauty products. The young women here can buy all these things themselves.

The links between poverty, prostitution, and HIV/AIDS were echoed time and again by female artisans.

Young single weavers, mostly in their twenties, told of receiving sexual propositions from men and of how their reactions have evolved since they started crafting baskets for sale. Because it diminishes financial want, "weaving assures me independence and hope for a better future," says Dévota Kabahire.

It means I'm able to determine the outcome of my life. I can defend myself against boys who want to sleep with me. No man can come and offer me money. I earn my own money, I can choose a partner and decide my own future.

Dévota said she has received many offers from men.

Boys often use money to entice girls. And if you end up having sex, most people don't use protection, so you risk being infected. But if a girl has money, she isn't attracted by material things, and so won't fall into men's trap. There are many boys who have tried to seduce me, but I'm quickly able to see through this and refuse them. Our earnings have a positive impact on HIV/AIDS prevention.

Although she is unmarried and only twenty-two, Athanasia Mukayandi, like Dévota, feels as though she requires nothing from men.

No one can lead me into error or tempt me once the baskets are sold. I can buy things that I want, like cosmetic products. If someone comes and tries to lie to me and tempt me, I can just say, "I'm satisfied with what I have."

Athanasia's ability to provide for herself sets her apart from her age-mates, and helps her avoid behavior that could jeopardize her health.

I can't compare myself to other young women who don't weave. It's when you don't have money that you're tempted and risk getting AIDS. But when you have money from weaving, you won't do something that could be dangerous, like having unprotected sexual intercourse.

Julienne Uwambajimana is another young weaver who recognizes that her economic activity places her in a very different financial situation from many of her friends.

Most of my friends who don't weave cannot buy clothes, lotion, and everything they need.

She is not obliged to leave her home in Ruhango to find work in the capital, one of the few places where self-sufficiency may be available to poor girls her age.

Young girls go to Kigali to be domestic workers in order to earn money. And sometimes they come back pregnant because they ask boys to buy them clothes or other things. So they sleep with them and get pregnant. If you are a house girl, you can also be raped. Or maybe you have sex with your boss because you need money or because he asks you to. All of these things can happen if you are a house girl.

The main cause of infection, she says, is prostitution. She gave a hypothetical example of how a girl could be infected with HIV.

Let's say you go to Gisenyi with your boyfriend and have a good time. He might give you money for a new outfit or makeup. After you accept that money, you aren't going to refuse to have sex with him. And if he has HIV/AIDS, you'll get it immediately.

She sees herself as being "on a different level."

We can purchase things for ourselves. We don't have time for prostitution or being involved in things that aren't important. We spend all of our time weaving. And when you are weaving, no boy is going to come and offer you a little money. This can't interest or excite you because you know that you are going to make your own money.

Rose believes that men seek out the easiest targets.

Men will offer you money in exchange for sex, particularly when you are poor. People try to take advantage of you when they know you have problems.

Men also try their luck pursuing weavers.

Men have offered to pay me to sleep with them. Boys think I look more attractive because I weave, and all of them come telling me nice things and flirting because they think I have money. They approach me because they want both sex and money; they think that I can also buy them a drink. But I can't accept them.

When asked if she ever accepted propositions from men, Rose replied,

"I was tempted," but explained that weaving has made her more decisive in her responses to men.

I refuse them with more vigor and confidence. How can men lie to me when I can provide what I need for myself and I am satisfied? I have pride now because I'm okay with what I have and don't have to look elsewhere. I'm also optimistic. Before I had nothing; now I have progressed and I look forward to the future. I've learned how to take care of myself on my own.

Promoting Awareness

In addition to reducing financial motives for women to engage in premarital or extramarital sex, weaving also provides an arena in which women can learn more about the disease. Cooperatives sometimes organize educational programs for their members. Also, because weavers are together in a group, they are able to keep up with events at their cellule and sector offices and so often learn of public sensitization initiatives or workshops they can attend.

Anatalia Niwemutima's ideas about the origins of AIDS changed when she started weaving.

I used to think HIV was caused by witchcraft, but now I know how it is transmitted and how to care for those who are infected without isolating them. I learned all this from the association through various meetings and by talking to the members.

This new knowledge prompted her to take action.

I have been tested three times and found that I am negative.

Although Françoise's weaving group in Ruhashya has not had formal information sessions directed specifically towards them, being a member makes her more likely to attend training programs in the area.

The association is always told about the schedule of events and activities in the community so we learn about what is going on and when there are going to be information sessions. So we can go to these and become better informed.

In their discussions and exchange of advice, HIV/AIDS is a topic Josephine and her fellow weavers bring up.

You can critique each other on different subjects. And also, if we think someone is resorting to prostitution, we will advise her stop so she won't get HIV.

The Dukundane group of weavers in Rwaniro has, among its objectives, the inclusion of HIV-positive residents and raising awareness of HIV/AIDS. Its leadership coordinated an effort to ensure that everyone in the cooperative, as well as in the wider community, knew their health status. François Ntambara is proud of his contribution to this effort.

Everyone in the cooperative, and most of the people around here, have been tested for HIV/AIDS. We requested this service from the district and they sent doctors from Rusatira. This was about a month ago, and yesterday counselors came to speak with the people who tested positive.

François thought that, of those tested, perhaps fourteen had tested positive. This represents an important achievement on the part of the cooperative, because it signifies that fourteen more people are conscious of their status and able to take measures so they do not infect others. In such a small community, this represents an extremely valuable milestone in preventing the spread of HIV.

A Persistent Need for Education

Although group membership has a clear impact on combating ignorance of HIV/AIDS, it is also evident that this in itself, even with opportunities to gain information from outside sources, is insufficient. Some weavers, several of whom are HIV-positive, make a particular effort to nurture openness, reducing stigma, and promoting a greater awareness of what HIV/AIDS is and how it is contracted. But some of the weavers who spoke of their efforts to educate say that much of what they say falls on deaf ears.

Rose (a pseudonym) changed the way she reacts to men, not only because they no longer present a financial temptation, but also because she had learned from her mistakes, which led her to have a child out of wedlock. Weavers have commented that condom use among rural youth is low. Although she was sexually active, protection was not even on Rose's mind.

I didn't know anything about condoms. I had heard about them, but had never seen one.

Rose also knew little of HIV/AIDS. She only learned the basic facts of transmission when she went to get tested while pregnant.

When I went for my test, I learned that it's transmitted sexually, through syringes or by local doctors who use the same knives or razor blades on multiple people. I didn't know this before I got tested. I had never had any sensitization about HIV/AIDS.

This knowledge has led her to take new precautions.

I went with my child's father to get tested again six months ago. This was the second time we've been tested. He used to do business here and then he moved. I couldn't trust him and that's why we took another test. The results were negative.

Rose now puts herself forth as an example of the potential consequences of pre-marital unprotected intercourse. She shares her knowledge and experience in order to guide her companions away from making her same mistakes.

Not all of the weavers have changed as I have. I sometimes try to advise them. The advice I give to weavers who accept to sleep with men for money is: Be motivated and don't get discouraged in weaving; Have safe sex.

Some men will lie to you and it's difficult for you to refuse them. They can seduce and flirt with you until you can't control yourself. There is no girl at this age who doesn't have a boyfriend. So have one boyfriend, be faithful to him, and use condoms.

But there are some who do not heed Rose's counsel.

There are those who understand and listen to you, but others just laugh and say I think that I'm smart and that I have changed so much. Young girls aren't interested in getting tested, unless they're going to live with their boyfriends or get married.

Despite all this, even Rose does not follow her own advice.

Even up till now, we have sex, but don't use condoms. I worry about getting pregnant again.

Although she believes her boyfriend is faithful, she knows she is putting herself at risk of HIV/AIDS. The knowledge level and openness of Rose and colleagues underlines the gaps in awareness that need to be formally addressed.

Five years have passed since Yvette (a pseudonym) discovered that she is HIV-positive. She believes it is her husband who passed the virus on to her. She now lives every day with the burden and fear of thinking that her spouse, who refuses to be tested and continues to be unfaithful, is likely infecting others.

I try to explain to my husband that he should be tested, but he doesn't want to go. He also still has sex with other women. I feel bad about this, but there's nothing I can do.

Yvette knows the women he sleeps with, but holds back from confronting them directly.

One of the women is a single mother with three children and the other one is a widow. I haven't told them that he might have HIV/AIDS. You see, when people are sharing a husband with you, they can't believe you. They'll think you're just saying things because you're jealous.

Yvette says she has tried "to use indirect ways to let them know."

For example, if I go to the hospital to get medicine, I might meet with other women who live near them. I'll ask them to tell the women they saw me taking medication. But then those women then pass a message back to me to say that their blood is immune to HIV/AIDS.

Aspects of Yvette's story are extremely distressing. First among them is her husband, who may well be endangering the lives of his multiple partners. Also notable is Yvette's sense of helplessness, or perhaps her lack of courage, to take measures to change the current situation.

I continue to live with my husband and I'm not happy. But I don't think that there's anything else I can do.

She follows advice from fellow weavers and keeps trying to convince her husband to be tested, and to refrain from having sex with other women. But she is not very optimistic. At the end of the interview, she requested our prayers.

I want you to pray for me, for my husband to go to the hospital and get tested.

According to Yvette, there are women among the weavers and in the wider community who resist HIV/AIDS education, are reluctant to discuss it openly, and avoid being tested. This is particularly common, she says, among single women.

Most of the people in the community want to learn more about HIV, but others don't. When women have children, they get tested. But single women don't think about this, and don't want to be tested. People need someone to push them to see if they are positive or negative. They should also be trained as weavers, so they can develop and support themselves.

I can't say that the weavers don't know about HIV/AIDS, but many of them are afraid of going to the hospital. When someone comes to a general meeting with proposals about testing, the women feel shy and don't want to hear about those ideas.

One source of comfort for Yvette is the fact that she no longer feels that she's an object of stigma.

People used to discriminate against me, and even against our children. They didn't want my children to play with theirs. Some people are still like this, but it isn't a general problem anymore. They've changed because many organizations come and teach people about HIV/AIDS.

Azelle (a pseudonym) uses her position as president of her association in Gitarama, and as an HIV-positive woman, to urge others to take the necessary precautionary measures.

Most of the women know that I'm HIV-positive. We've spoken about this amongst ourselves. When we are sitting together, we talk about HIV and discuss how it's transmitted. And as president, I can tell the other weavers how bad HIV is. I can teach them how to prevent it and advise them to go to the hospital to see if they have HIV. For example, when someone wants to talk about me and says, "Did you know that she's sick?" I can reply, "Yes I'm sick, but you also should go to get tested!"

She sees the importance of being open about her health.

I've discovered that it's not good to keep your personal problems to yourself. I'm happy to share my personal life, and I think this is helpful for other weavers.

Azelle has also tried to address the stigma associated with being HIV-positive.

I explain to them that someone who has HIV doesn't have to be kept at arm's length, that they can be sharp and active, walk around, be busy and proud. And I tell them that they don't have to be afraid of people who have HIV/ AIDS, that we are normal.

Because she considers prevalence rates to be high, her efforts take on even greater significance.

In my small group of weavers, I know of five who are very sick. In Abahuje, many of the women have HIV. And in the community in general, there are many people who have HIV.

Some other women are as open as Azelle. But she also recognizes that many others who are infected live in ignorance, and some are in denial.

Some of the other women who have HIV also feel free to talk about how they survive and how it's transmitted. They are on medication and don't worry if others know. What is worrying is that some who have not been tested are not interested and don't care about HIV. They don't want to listen to our advice. They don't know if they are positive or not. There are also people who know that they have it, but don't want others to know, and don't want to go to the hospital to take medicine.

Marc (a pseudonym), Azelle's husband, admits that his infidelity brought HIV/AIDS into their home. He was at first reticent to have his blood checked but eventually understood the importance, for the sake of his wife and children, of being aware of his status. Yet he says that "other men still have that problem and don't want to go and get tested." Marc now works with his wife to sensitize the weavers and the community as a whole.

Instead of staying at home and keeping quiet about my status, I decided to join an HIV/AIDS association in Byimana funded by CARE. Also, when the women are here weaving, I sometimes take my medicine right in front of them, to purposefully show them that I'm HIV-positive, and that I'm open about it.

He says he also does this to deflect interest from women.

I also do this because some women might see me as a rich man and want to have sex with me. But the girls here who see me taking my medicine won't be interested in having sex with me anymore.

Living with HIV/AIDS

For people living with HIV/AIDS, weaving has provided their sustenance, security, and hope for a long and healthy future. They can now afford the nutritious diet required to sustain an anti-retroviral regimen, pay for treatment of opportunistic infections, and support themselves when they fall ill.

Yvette knows the importance of eating well and is glad that she has the resources to do so.

The money from weaving enables me to buy porridge, sugar, fruit, and vegetables. These are important to my life as someone who has HIV/AIDS.

For Azelle, the money she earns from weaving is crucial in her fight to maintain her health.

The money helps us as people living with HIV. I can buy myself what I need. Since I started to weave, I haven't lacked anything. When I get sick, I can take care of myself. I can buy sugar or fruit, which are important for my health. I can't cultivate, but I hire someone else. Weaving is helping me so much.

And her illness does not become a burden to others.

My extended family is also happy because I don't have to depend on them.

Azelle credits crafting baskets with saving her life.

If I wasn't weaving, I think I'd be dead, or very much alone. I'd have no way of taking care of myself.

But Azelle is far from alone. Instead, she and hundreds of other weavers are drawing strength from each other to broaden their horizons, sharpen their skills, and enter the public domain with a confidence they could never have imagined a few years ago.

CHAPTER 7

At the Forefront of Their Communities

Female basket weavers are now reaching out much further than the borders of their land, or the membership of their weaving group, and into their communities at large. They can look after themselves and their families, and also friends and neighbors. When they purchase food and goods from their neighbors and pay them for help on their farms, their earnings from basket sales spread among other residents in their areas and are beneficial to development, even at the regional level.

In Rwanda, due to strong policies and mechanisms directed towards assuring female participation in governance, women have become visible and vocal in the political arena. Through Rwanda's successive administrative units—the cellule, sector, district, and province—constitutional guarantees, and a quota system that reserves seats for women, they are becoming a force to reckon with. Yet the reality is that for a poor rural woman with a low level of education, standing for election to the executive committee of her cellule is already off her radar and the least of her priorities.

Gainful employment has made women who become weavers more presentable, independent, and confident. They are, as a result, now much more likely to be involved in local government and public affairs. Taken as models for other women to emulate, their communities seek them out as representatives. The weavers feel capable of responding to these calls, are ready to contribute their perspectives, and eager to make their opinions heard. Many now hold elected posts as the *chargé* responsible for social affairs, economic affairs, and development on cellule executive committees; as representatives on local women's or youth councils; and as *inyangamugayo*, judges, in their local *gacaca* jurisdictions. Of the 360 weavers interviewed for this book, a majority hold such posts. Based on their comments describing the links between taking up weaving and taking on leadership, it is fair to assume that most of these women would not have the titles they do today were it not for weaving.

Impacting the Wider Community: Spurring Economic Development and Helping Neighbors

The business of weaving in Gitarama and Butare benefits the individual weavers and their families, but also has a wider economic effect on surrounding communities. Approximately three thousand weavers bring in tens of thousands of Rwandese francs to their areas each month, thus dramatically increasing the flow of cash into and within these rural economies. Weavers spend the money they earn within their localities; they purchase foodstuffs and household items at the local stores, pay for local labor, and rent land form local land owners.

The conglomerations of shops scattered around Ruhango district would be much smaller were it not for weaving, said Eugenie Nyanzira.

Businesses and commercial centers have developed and prospered because of weaving. The business people are happy because they know they will sell things and make a lot of money, particularly on days when women are paid.

In areas with large numbers of craftswomen, improvements in the living conditions of individual families are multiplied across numerous non-weaving households, thus impacting quality of life and coping mechanisms at the community level.

If an umudugudu *has ten or fifty weavers, it means that every month many homes are receiving money and resolving their problems.*

Séraphine Mukamugema told of how weavers' income trickles out among area residents.

When we buy sisal, for example, the money goes to men who are not weavers. We also pay people to cultivate our fields.

The ability to lend money to those living around them was described time and again by weavers like Séraphine Mukarubwera as an important way in which basket making helps others.

I once lent 10,000 francs to my neighbor who had to have a C-section, which her health insurance would not cover. This family was very poor. They reimbursed me 4,000 francs. For the rest, instead of paying me in money, the husband helps me cultivate twice a week. I felt good that she felt able to ask me for money, that I had it, and was able save the life of her child. She has had more children. Even though she has to pay me in different ways, we are very close friends.

The health of neighbors and their children is also immensely important to Espérance Mukanyandwi. She is glad that she can step in to make sure that an ailing child can access healthcare.

It might happen that my neighbor has a sick child, and she needs to borrow money from me to take the child to the hospital. She'll pay me back later. I'm pleased that I can intervene.

In addition to her ability to loan money, Françoise Mukamana also welcomes the opportunity to teach her neighbors to weave.

I feel that I've become useful to my neighbors who don't weave. If someone in my community needs money, I can give or lend them some. This gives me standing in my area. One time, I was asked to teach others how to weave. There were sixty participants from my cellule and from other cellules. They all respect me now. And it's a pleasure for me to know that I've done something for my community.

Breaking Down the Barriers to Leadership

When asked to discuss the relationship between weaving and taking on leadership roles, many weavers began by speaking of how the simple fact of gainful employment and resulting income has facilitated their participation in local decision-making bodies. That they are working women and financially independent spurs others to admire and respect them. They are also better dressed and cleaner than other women in their localities, and this carries a great deal of weight.

Joseline Kanyange can feel a change in the strength of her voice, both in how she speaks and in how she is heard.

Because I have a source of income, I am respected in the society and within the association. I can speak with boldness about my choices and opinions because I am no longer a beggar. I feel I have value in my family and society.

As Séraphine Mukarubwera explains, feeling comfortable about the way in which others see you is a prerequisite for community involvement.

Weaving helps the women to be sharp, and not to be isolated or shy. Before, the women weren't clean and didn't have enough money to buy soap to wash their bodies or clothes; they were embarrassed to be in public because they were dirty. But now, they are dressed well and so they feel fine leaving their homes and being active. Weaving helps them to participate in government activities and planning.

Espérance stated very clearly how a person's relative wealth or poverty can play into the voting process.

When everyone sits together to vote, we select someone depending on her appearance, cleanliness, and occupation. If there are two people, and one is dirty and one is clean, people will choose the clean person to represent them. And we here are clean because of the money that we get from weaving.

Dévota Kabahire put forward a similar explanation as to why weavers are drawn into positions as local officials.

The president of our association is a woman and there are others who have responsibilities in the cellule and sector. This is linked to weaving because in rural areas, we can't elect someone who isn't presentable and doesn't wear nice clothes. But when you are neatly dressed and clean, people will solicit you to lead them. It is working women who fulfill this condition.

A *gacaca* judge, Françoise attributes her ability to take on this position to the money she earns from weaving.

I used to be looked upon as poor. And when you are poor, you are hesitant about appearing in public because you are not proud of yourself and you know that you don't command respect from others. But now, I feel better because I'm economically okay. I feel free and capable of taking on this role. To be given a role as a local authority or leader requires the trust and respect of the community. People have confidence that I can represent the survivors in my cellule.

For Joseline, it is not only the fact that leaders look "smart" that allows them to stand before others, but also that they are "empowered."

Economically, weavers are more empowered than non-weavers. This also leads to political empowerment. Because women weavers are no longer totally dependent on their husbands, they therefore command respect from them and from society. Women weavers have become vocal and can advocate for their rights.

Louise Byukusenge, who weaves peace baskets in Kigali, clarified why dependency constrains a woman's voice.

Weaving has helped me to become an independent-minded person. I used to feel that I had to obey whatever I was told, without question. This was mainly because I was dependent on other people economically. This has changed, and I can speak my mind clearly because I know I won't be affected in any way. I know that I will not lack food or shelter as a result of what I say.

Godelieve Mukagatera in Ruhashya wants to see more women weavers engage with local politics.

Where I live, there are many who participate in government and in the gacaca *courts. Of the* gacaca *judges in my area, four out of seven are women, and three of these are weavers. Among the* abunzi *(mediators) in my* cellule*, four out of twelve are women. I'm one of them, and I'm the only weaver. I feel that it is important for me to participate in government. You cannot expect good governance if you aren't ready to take part yourself. To be a mediator, you must be elected. This means that people in the community must trust you.*

Self-reliance sets Tharcisse Kaberuka's female colleagues apart from other women.

People underestimate women because they are seen as appendages of their husbands. But through weaving, women become productive, self-sufficient, and gain respect. They participate in governance. For example, there are some female weavers who are cellule responsables*. There's one who's in charge of health at the* cellule *level. Our president is well-known and is always invited to meetings to share ideas. She's very well respected by the authorities and the community. If there are meetings—for example, about economic development in the area—she's the one who will go to represent us.*

What starts as a shift in relationships between husbands and wives carries over to the status of women outside, as Glorioza Uwamahoro commented.

In our association we have so many women who are involved in different leadership positions such as in gacaca *and in the local women's council.*

Joseph Ndamage has seen these changes occur in the women he taught to weave.

Economic empowerment results in political empowerment, and leads to decision-making. The women have become stronger financially through the baskets and are progressing well. They have a say in their homes because they are liberated. They make decisions in their families alongside their husbands. Women weavers are far ahead of non-weavers. Some of the women in our association are community leaders. For example, we have one gacaca *judge and one* umudugudu *leader for social welfare.*

The gender balance in Séraphine Mukandamage's home was seen as a model for other couples to follow, which helped secure her appointment as the person in charge of social affairs on the Ntenyo executive committee.

I was chosen because people took me as someone who is capable of taking on these responsibilities and of accomplishing all the duties of the position. And they saw that I could teach others to weave, that I'm healthy, and that I could teach them how to be healthy as well. Also, they try to choose people who have gender in their homes. By this, I mean equality in the home, people who know that it's wrong to discriminate on the basis of sex. In such a house, a wife is a partner and can deal with problems, just as a man can.

I fee confident and equal to my husband. No one came to point out to us that this is how things should be. We just sat down together, talked, and came to this understanding. Weaving is important because it helps me put this idea of balance into practice. I have the capacity to support our family and so I can make decisions on anything that I want.

Overcoming Fear and Gaining Confidence

The knowledge that they are respected by others and capable of participating in decision-making within the family and community gives weavers a greater sense of self-worth, which reinforces their ability to take on positions of leadership. The high level of public recognition they receive also impacts how they see themselves. "Weaving," said Espérance, "makes us feel good and boosts our morale."

It gives us the power to hold leadership positions. Local authorities are pleased to see us involved in these activities. Sometimes we are introduced to visitors, and the officials say, "These are the weavers of the area." This makes us proud and confident.

The buzz that surrounds Vestine Mukandikwe and her fellow weavers when they go to church in Byimana gives them immense self-satisfaction.

Sitting amidst large groups of women, it is hard for weavers to feel shy; any anxiety over being in public gatherings quickly disappears. The associations and cooperatives are spaces in which women can develop management and leadership skills. When a weaver takes on a position as president, secretary, or treasurer of her weaving group, she suddenly begins to see herself as capable of mobilizing, organizing, and directing others. Craftswomen also are given an opportunity to develop their abilities to speak in front of others. With women from their same background who share their occupation, they have little reason to feel intimidated about sharing their opinions. Such experience diminishes their fear of becoming a local official and standing before the members of their cellule or sector.

Timidity before large audiences is a thing of the past for Joseline.

I never used to go in public or talk in front of large congregations. I used to be shy but am not anymore. Speaking in the association was a milestone for us; it made it possible to be bold and to speak in public.

Godansi Mukabahizi says weaving has enabled her to "stand up and talk in public, to know my rights and advocate for them." And Glorioza's inhibitions are also gradually fading.

I used to fear people and speaking in public. This has lessened, and I believe will completely disappear.

The barriers against speaking out are not only personal, but also cultural. Louise thinks employment is making such obstacles crumble, allowing a twenty-year-old girl like her to blossom.

In Rwandese culture, girls weren't supposed to speak in public or oppose men in any way. Weaving has opened our minds, and we have gone beyond cultural barriers.

Weaving cooperatives have become prominent groups in civil society as well as in the business world. They are active and aware of all major local events and have become an advertisement for women's economic and social development. Leaders pay attention to their activities and maintain contact with their members, putting civic and political appointments within their reach.

Glorioza has formed connections with the many new people she has come to know through weaving.

All our political and religious leaders know us and we know them. They are helpful to us professionally, and even when we have an individual problem.

Feeling comfortable around local leaders is one step Athanasia Mukayandwi has taken towards becoming one herself.

Before joining the association, I felt intimidated by local authorities, and many others had this same tendency. But because we are in an association, we aren't afraid of them anymore. And once that fear leaves you, you yourself can consider becoming an authority. If you are a leader of the association, you can't be afraid of other leaders.

The opportunity to meet and interact with officials has made Athanasia see them as approachable.

According to Théodore Rutagengwa, another reason these women are active citizens is because weavers are always abreast of what is going on in the area.

Through being in the association, they always know when meetings are going to take place. When they go, they are confident and proud.

As members of their cooperatives, weavers are also learning how to be businesswomen, which requires them to learn how to hold their own, even when they are far away from their familiar home turf.

They have to travel to find a market. They can't come across a market if they don't move around. Weaving leads them to venture outside of their own areas.

The weavers meet with government bodies and business partners to discuss their crafts. This gives them exposure to the world beyond their neighborhoods, and is one reason why Grâce Mujawamariya says, "Weaving makes us more self-assured."

We have always thought of the world as a place for educated people. But women weavers have realized their value in the society because they contribute to the national income and to the well-being of their families.

They have ceased to be kitchen women, and have traveled widely both within Rwanda and abroad. Presidents of weaving associations represent their members at different forums, negotiate and advocate for them. The peace basket has taken one woman, Pascasie, to the U.S. and another to Belgium. We have met with RIEPA, AVEGA, and Gahaya Links to discuss markets for baskets. Society has always viewed women as second-class citizens, but not anymore.

Their wide recognition, and the fact that their members are organized, allows them to take part in periodic workshops and training sessions.

Male weavers, and the spouses of women weavers, see in women natural capacities to lead well, but some wonder if political leadership ranks high among their aspirations. Having watched the women who serve in his cooperative in Rwaniro, François Ntambara gave reasons why he thinks "women are definitely better leaders than men."

I don't know if it's because women didn't work before, but now they are working and they have so much motivation. Their thoughts are good and they are honest. I've observed their working methods and habits. When we are with them, we exchange ideas and our discussions get us somewhere and result in something. Women aren't sly; they're straightforward. But men think that they are bright and witty. If a lady tells me something, I know I can trust her.

Other male weavers, including Vincent Burasazwe, also have a high regard for women's involvement in politics and public life.

Women's involvement in politics is healthy because they can lead the people. Most of the weavers are sharp; they can contest any position and win.

Given women's preoccupation with looking after their families, Vincent has noticed that for some weavers, their time and energy feels too precious for them to serve as officials.

They are constantly thinking of how many baskets they can finish in a month.

Théodore made a similar observation, saying that holding an elected position is not necessarily a priority for his wife or her co-workers.

CHAPTER 8

An Urban Context

THE BRACELET MAKERS IN KIGALI

In July 2007 Fair Winds Trading embarked on a new project, in conjunction with *O, The Oprah Magazine*, which trained women in Rwanda's capital, Kigali, to make high-quality bracelets using a variety of imported beads. Thirty of those trained and employed as beaders in this project were interviewed to see how their experience compared with that of the weavers.

Some of the women beaders joined the program after an initial vocational training course at Women for Women, which taught basic skills in weaving, beading, knitting, or sewing. Others had been taught at the Cesar Center, an NGO training center in Kigali. Even those who came with some knowledge of beading required new knowledge, more sophisticated technique, and considerable support to satisfy the demands of the intended upscale market for these bracelets. Two kinds of bracelets were produced: a simpler version for which beaders were paid 3,000 francs, and a more sophisticated style paying 5,000 francs at the end of each day. Some of the younger women are able to complete two of the simpler bracelets per day, thereby earning 6,000 francs per day.

The women were taught and supervised by Dean Ericson, the president and Rwanda representative of Fair Winds Trading, in a house in Kimihurura where they were also given lunch. They ordinarily start beading at 9:00 a.m., with a lunch break of one hour, and continued until 5:00 p.m. The women belong to different associations, and most of them are HIV-positive. Some of the younger women were selected because their mothers are HIV-positive and are not well enough to work themselves.

The findings, in terms of the impact of earning an income and of working in a group, are not very different from those related to the weavers. The main difference is that the beaders, because they are based in the capital, tend to be, on the whole, better-educated than the weavers in the rural areas, especially the younger women who have aspirations of going to university. In addition, they place a greater emphasis on the importance of a varied diet, and of being able to eat more fruit and drink more milk on a regular basis. They also earn much more than the weavers, and all expressed great satisfaction with the level of pay. And because they earn more, most are able to put some money aside every week.

"Beading Has Solved So Many of Our Problems"

The women's sense of relief and pride in earning their own income is palpable. Like the weavers, their priorities are sending their children to school, taking care of household expenses, paying for medical needs, taking out health coverage for themselves and their children, eating more carefully on a more regular basis, and paying rent. The fact that they are financially independent makes others in their neighborhood look upon them differently, they said, and to respect them more.

Laurence (a pseudonym) can hardly believe her luck. Aged forty-five, she was previously unemployed, and with only three years of primary education she had little chance of a job with a decent salary. She lost her husband and five of her six children in the genocide. A son, who is now twenty-two, survived. She herself was raped then and became pregnant as a result. She has a thirteen-year-old child as a consequence of the rape and later discovered that she was HIV-positive, another result of the rape. In addition to her two children, she has adopted a nine-year-old orphan. She came to the project through Women for Women.

> *We love this work, and the way in which we work is good for us. We are very well paid. We just pray that there will always be buyers for our products.*

She found it difficult to compare her previous situation with her current status.

> *My life before and after I started beading is really incomparable. Before, I felt I was nothing. I didn't earn anything and with my illness, I was so unhappy. But now I see myself as being on the same level as civil servants because I earn as much as they do, and I go to work every morning.*

> *We can buy things for our homes. We can send children to school and buy them clothes. I'm taking ARVs and feel strong and healthy. I can take care of myself and really don't have any health problems. As for the young girls who work here, they can pay for English and computer classes. Some of them have finished high school and hope that if the market continues, they'll be able to pay to go to university.*

Laurence's oldest son had to drop out of school to look after her when she became seriously ill. But he has now returned to school.

> *It's my work here that allows me to afford his school fees.*

Her daughter of thirteen, and the youngest, also attend school.

> *They all study in schools that are far from our home in Kimironko. They all need money for transport everyday, and it's because of this work that I can manage this.*

Laurence is especially pleased, and proud, that she is able to save money on a weekly basis.

On most days, I make 3,000 francs. I use 1,500 to buy food for the house and for my transport. Then I keep the remaining 1,500. At the end of the week I deposit 5,000 francs into my bank account at Banque Populaire and 2,500 into my account at Ikingi Savings and Credit Cooperative. I've had my Banque Populaire account for five years now, but there are times when it has been completely empty. I now have 150,000 francs saved in this account. I try not to spend this money, and save it for really important things, mostly for my children's school fees. I save this money so I can be certain that when they're starting a new school year, I'm able to pay for everything they need. It's true that at times, the money almost finishes, but slowly I earn it back. I have 50,000 in my account with Ikingi. I use this money for essentials and withdraw money regularly.

While most of Laurence's income comes from making bracelets, she earns extra cash from the local markets by making other jewelry, beaded pens, and paper necklaces together with her children, spending some of the money and adding the rest to her savings.

She understood the value of saving when she became seriously ill.

I really had no way of surviving. If I had tried to put money aside, my son would have been able to stay in school. But he had to stop studying to earn money. I learned a lesson from this. I also save because I've seen that if you have a lot of money at home, you are always tempted to buy things that are not important. But when your money is in the bank, you buy only what you know is essential.

Marguerite Uwimabera, a widow, must look after seven children, ranging in age from twenty-eight to ten. With only six years of primary education, her options, like those of Laurence, were limited, and she was barely able to make ends meet as a small-scale trader.

For women who don't have a job or profession, it is difficult to earn money and to provide for their families. This is particularly hard for widows. I had no way of making enough money even for the bare essentials. That's why the training we received as beaders, and our work, are so important.

In a month, I can earn 60,000 francs from beading. I don't have any other source of income. With my earnings, I am able to pay for healthcare coverage for myself and for my children. I can also save some money in my bank account. Beading has increased my hope in the future. I'm now able to pay my children's school fees without the problems that I used to have.

Léonie Karire was a young woman of twenty-seven when her husband perished in 1994, leaving her in charge of their four children, now aged eighteen, sixteen, fourteen, and twelve. Even though she was, as she said, "working just to feed my children," she was able to hold out, more or less, until 1999, doing different kinds of small business.

Then my business went downhill, especially when the market shifted from town to Kimironko. I tried to continue my business, but I was working just to put food on the table. At the end of 2005, I stopped for good. My circumstances became terrible. I had nothing to do and no income. Sometimes, I had a hard time even to feed my children. All I had was what I got from some well-wishers.

She has come a long way since.

These days, I earn either 5,000 francs a day, or 6,000 francs when I make two of the bracelets that fetch 3,000 [francs] each.

The money has had dramatic consequences for my family. We eat three times a day, including milk and fruits for my children. I buy nice clothes for my children, so they are not shy around other children. I'm sure my children used to feel embarrassed around others, because they didn't have good clothes like them. Sometimes, our neighbors tell us that we are lucky, because they know how things have changed in our lives. Some of them are becoming jealous of us.

With beading, I can satisfy all my needs, and still put some money in the bank. In a week, I might save a maximum of 10,000 francs, or a minimum of 5,000 francs, but mostly 10,000. So I hope that in the future, I will build up my capital and start a new business if this beading work finishes. If this work becomes permanent, we will be like bank employees or other people who are well-paid.

Pascasie Uwimana, sixty-one, used to make beaded items at home, and her children took her products to craft shops. A widow, she had six children, but four were soldiers and were killed during the genocide.

Before I started this beading, I was really poor. I was always dirty because I had no change of clothes, and I was so thin. I was always thinking about how my children would survive. But I couldn't come up with a solution. So for me, what's happened is really a miracle, because now I can pay the rent on my house myself, we can eat three times a day at home, and eat all kinds of food. And I'm able to give my children what they require for school and buy them clothes. I'm also able to visit my daughter, who is in a boarding school. I have even managed to pay healthcare coverage for myself and my children. And I'm able to save 10,000 francs a week. It's wonderful that I can resolve all my problems at home and take care of my children.

If they find a permanent market for the bracelets and we can continue working like this, then maybe my dream of owning my own home will come true.

It is a huge relief for Chantal Uwantege, with three young children to feed, educate, and bring up, that she does not have to wait until the end of the month for her husband's salary. She graduated from high school and married young. Like so many women faced with economic pressures, she tried her hand at business.

I couldn't always make a profit. And when I needed some money to buy food for my children, I'd take some of the money from my business. I went bankrupt twice and so I had to close my business. There never used to be a guarantee that I could make 3,000 francs a day, but today I can.

As an illustration of how beading had brought about "a huge transformation" in her life, Chantal spoke at length about the quality and quantity of food they eat now, compared to the past.

The food we ate wasn't very good. I just used to make sure that I could put something to eat on the table. We had no choice about the food. We just ate normal Rwandese food like beans and rice. All I could be sure about, was that we would eat something. Maybe we would have meat once a week.

We eat much better these days, vary our diet, and are healthy. Having a varied diet is important for children. On Mondays and Tuesdays, we eat meat, Wednesdays and Thursdays we eat fish, and on Friday meat or fish. Fruit is very important for children, and I always tried to buy them some fruit. But now instead of buying a half kilo of passion fruit or prunes, which wasn't really enough, I can buy a whole kilo. All of this because of the money I earn here.

Chantal's children have drawn other benefits.

My first two children are in boarding schools. I'm now able to visit them regularly and take them everything they need. I can also help to pay their school fees, thanks to this work.

My children used to find it hard to study. I'd pay the minimum amount of school fees necessary for them to start the school year, but they wouldn't have all the materials that the school asked of them. But now, with my savings, when they start school, I'm certain that I can pay for their fees and for everything else. Boarding school is expensive, but we're managing. My life is simply not what it used to be.

The mother of four children, Julienne Umugwaneza is divorced; two of the children live with her, and two live with their father. At one point poverty had forced Julienne to send her son to her aunt's home.

I was in a really bad situation. I couldn't pay the rent, feed my children, give them the basic materials for school.... I decided to take one of my children to my aunt's place. I couldn't take care of two children, especially the older one who was in school.

But with the money I earn from this beading project, I can do everything I want, something I never thought I would achieve in my life. I took my son back to my house because I can offer him everything he must have for his schooling. I am to able to send the young one to a private nursery school, to pay the rent, to give my children nice food, even milk on a regular basis, and to go to the market everyday and buy them fruits. Every day I save 3,000 francs, that is I put 15,000 francs in the bank every week. I thank God with all my heart for this job because it has turned my life around.

What I want, above all else, is to go to university. It's my primary ambition, so when I have enough money to pay for university, it's what I'll do.

Joseline Ntihemuka is one of the younger and better educated women. She graduated from high school in 2006 but then found herself jobless. A genocide survivor, she lives with her elderly mother who does not work, and with her two younger sisters. They had no choice but to look to the Fund to Assist Survivors of the Genocide (FARG) and AVEGA, as well as to others.

But now I earn my own money. And with that money, I can look after my family. I'm able to buy food for our home, and can even afford to purchase meat and to buy milk regularly for my sisters. I can afford the materials my sisters need for school, and for myself, I paid to take courses in English and to take computer classes.

I've opened a bank account at the Commercial Bank of Rwanda. I can deposit money into my account every week. If I've beaded the 3,000-franc bracelets, I can deposit between 5,000 and 7,000 francs in my account. And when I've made the 5,000-franc bracelets, I can deposit 10,000.

What really makes me happy is that I've taken over responsibility for my family.

Joseline is busy looking to the future.

I have other plans in mind for my future goals. I think that with this work, I can accomplish them. My biggest project is to continue studying and go to university. With the money that I earn here, and if this work is permanent, I'll be able to pay for university, just as I've been able to pay for English and computer classes. My life is so different now. I can't imagine what I would have become were it not for this work.

Marie-Rose Mukambasabire, who lives with her mother and two younger brothers, also depended on donations given to her mother by acquaintances and charities. She is twenty-six, single, and has completed her high schooling.

Since I started this beading work, there's been a great shift in my life. I can buy food and everything we need at home. I can buy clothes for my brothers and for my mother. I can also purchase school materials for my brothers. We don't wait for others and rely on donations in order to ensure our survival. And the way we eat is good because our diet is varied; each day we eat something different. We eat fruit and lots of other things that we didn't eat before. And with all of these things that I do with my money, I am still able to put aside 10,000 francs each week to save.

I see a huge gap between me and my former schoolmates who are unemployed. They consider me to be a rich girl. They come to tell me when they have problems and need money. I'm happy when I can help them resolve their problems. This also shows the benefits of this work.

I think that if all girls my age had good jobs as I do, the spread of HIV/AIDS would diminish. Most girls are infected because they fall into the trap of men who offer them material things.

Louise (a pseudonym), twenty-two, left high school after two years when her mother, who was raped during the genocide, died in 2002, leaving Louise and her older sister to look after their younger sister who is HIV-positive. With no source of income other than 30,000 francs they receive from the contributions their father had paid towards social security, and conscious of the special needs of their sister, they too went from one benefactor to another. Her greatest pride is that they no longer "require any assistance."

I earn enough money for myself and my sisters. This is a good job, and we like it very much. We are very well paid.

I'm pleased that I can take on all the responsibilities for my family. I can buy nice clothes for my sisters and myself; and you can even see how nicely I've been able to do my hair. I can also afford fruits, milk, meat, and a variety of other foods. But the best thing I did in my life, which makes feel so good, is that I'm able to take my younger sister to the hospital and buy her ARVs.

We can also put some money aside. Now, we save all the money from the Social Security Fund. At home, we use only the money I earn from here. I hope that the money we are saving will allow my sister and me to get involved with another project, and that she will have something to do.

"My Social Life Has Changed Tremendously"

Like the weavers, the beaders come from different regions of the country, have different backgrounds, and include both younger and older women. What they have in common is extreme poverty, and the fact that most of them are HIV-positive. Their workplace enables them to establish a new social network which makes them feel less isolated, marginalized, and burdened with the stigma of HIV/AIDS. They share problems and give each other advice. In particular, those who are HIV-infected counsel the others to test for HIV/AIDS, and those who are not infected encourage those who are to talk about their illness and to feel less frightened and alone.

Laurence looks forward to leaving home in the morning.

Some days there are so many things going on in your head that you don't want to talk to anyone. But as soon as you get here, the other women start asking you what's wrong, and eventually you are able to talk and forget about your problems. It really comforts you. Being together helps us a lot and fights against isolation. When you are alone, you can have negative thoughts. This activity has really changed our lives.

Knowing she will have company even if she falls ill is source of comfort.

Even if we get sick, we're optimistic that we'll get better and come back to work. And if I fall ill, colleagues will come to visit me because now they all can afford the transport to do this. My social life has changed tremendously. Before, if relatives or colleagues were sick, I'd be too ashamed to visit them without being able to take something to offer. But now, I have no reason to be ashamed. I go to visit and take fruit or juice. I've become a normal person. Before I was isolated and felt marginalized.

Earning a regular income has given Marguerite self-confidence, which comes in part from the way she thinks others look upon her.

Those who live around me now consider me to be an important woman who earns a regular income. They respect me more than before.

Being surrounded by others has helped her come out of her shell.

I've become more social because we work as a group. I've gotten to know my co-workers and we discuss many different issues. We give each other advice. I find that being together is helpful for all the members. When a woman earns an income, it can also help to prevent HIV/AIDS because she needn't prostitute herself in order to earn some money. She has what she needs.

The younger women like Marie-Rose feel privileged to be working alongside older and more experienced women.

They offer us advice. We make jokes as we are beading, and we learn so much from each other.

One of the things that HIV-positive women learn, said Louise, is "to be more open to other people."

We are there for those with HIV/AIDS. We try to encourage them. Because we trust each other, they tell us the truth about AIDS. And slowly, they've learned to let their guard down.

And because of the friendship that exists between us, if someone finishes before the others, she helps her colleagues because we don't like anyone to go back home without money. This also contributes to reconciliation. We are a mixed group, as far as ethnicity is concerned. But if anyone has a problem, we try to help her without looking to see which group she belongs to.

But the advice is reciprocal, as Julienne noted.

Those who are infected urge us to take the HIV test, reminding us that they are still alive because they found out that their status, take drugs and try to be disciplined.

Chantal does not like to miss a single beading session.

If I don't come to work one day, although I might stay at home and rest, which is good, I miss the atmosphere of being in the group at work and sitting with the others.

Given their financial gains, beaders are understandably anxious about the market for their products. They worry that the demand might dwindle, making it difficult to justify continued employment.

Chapter 9

Challenges and Recommendations

The weavers interviewed by African Rights expressed their appreciation for the profound changes that have occurred in their lives and in those of their families since they began to earn an income from their craft. But change and transformation take time. And so they spoke, at the same time, about the difficulties they continue to face in their work, their communities, and families. They reflected the belief that there is a collective will to address these issues and to bring about lasting solutions.

Therefore, one of the most valuable aspects of the study was the opportunity for the weavers to voice their valid concerns and to articulate the challenges still to be met. They identified obstacles to be overcome in order to improve both the quality and the quantity of the products regardless of style of basket, materials used or location in which they are produced. Their suggestions and recommendation will be integrated into the ongoing development of the income-generating program in order to address the impediments that were identified.

Perceptions of a Fluctuating and Unstable Market

Although the weavers who produce baskets for Macy's deliver and sell their products regularly, there is an undercurrent anxiety about the future, and whether there will be buyers tomorrow. When baskets are rejected for reasons of quality, this is sometimes interpreted to mean that the market is unstable or saturated. Whether real or imagined, these worries reveal a sense of economic vulnerability and precariousness that is difficult to dispel. While a stable market cannot be guaranteed over the long term, it is important for the weavers to understand that this is currently not a risk. Continuous training and re-training will ensure that they are able to sell what they produce. At the same time, the weavers expressed the urgent need for the Government of Rwanda to begin looking into alternative profitable business opportunities for poor rural women over the longer term.

Developing Skills: Training, Trainers and Trainees

Ongoing training was emphasized as a priority for the weavers, and for continuing to build the skills of the trainers as new styles and techniques are introduced. Those women whose baskets were initially rejected, and who then received training to improve their skills, understand the power of training and the heightened pride in their work and self-respect that comes with it. Training of trainers and of the weavers needs to be strengthened and expanded in order to ensure that all weavers, whatever the style of the baskets they produce, can improve both the quality and quantity of their products.

Nowhere to Weave and Meet: Weaving Centers

A suitable meeting place was one of the most consistent requests. Many weaving groups do not have a sheltered space where they can weave together in comfort; therefore, they gather under trees or in open spaces, unprotected from rain or heat. Government-funded weaving centers are insufficient to cater to the thousands of weavers. The weavers shared a clear concept of what such structures should provide, including individual secure cubbies where they can store their baskets and materials overnight, shelves for displaying products for sale, and one large room where they can work in groups rather than a number of smaller ones.

The Expense and Scarcity of Raw Materials

Raw materials used to make baskets (particularly sisal, black banana fiber, and strong papyrus branches) are scarce and expensive. There is a need for adequate transportation to bring materials from other districts. The same high quality of the dyes and the spectrum of colors used in the production of the baskets needs to be available to all weavers, regardless of location and style of basket woven. This, in turn, nurtures ongoing creativity and artistic expression.

Capacity Building for Associations, Cooperatives, and Partners

The need for courses in financial management and accounting—to build on the rudimentary bookkeeping that has been learned—was an urgent request, particularly for cooperative and association treasurers. This would have the added benefit of strengthening the credit and loan systems that have already been established.

Dissemination of Important Information in a Structured Manner

The weaving associations and groups provide a unique opportunity for awareness-raising, for knowledge-building, and for information-dissemination to improve and expand life skills. In ordinary daily interactions among the artisans these issues are discussed and debated in an informal and anecdotal way. The work setting is ideal for workshops on violence against women, HIV/AIDS prevention, voluntary testing and treatment, reproductive health, laws that protect women against violence and promote women's rights, nutrition, hygiene, literacy, child care, the importance of educating girls, and household budget and resource management.

Violence Against Women

Given the nature and timescale of the study, it was not possible to gather in-depth information about such a personal and sensitive issue as violence against women in Rwanda. There is a pressing need for further, action-oriented research into the extent and nature of such violence and its impact on women's lives, as well as practical and workable recommendations and follow-up actions in conjunction with, for example, the police, justice officials, local government officials and women's organizations.

A Multi-Purpose Skills Training Center

The rapid construction of a multi-purpose learning/community center that could host training in a variety of technical skills, as well as address life-skills training and social education, could meet many of the needs and concerns articulated by the interviewees. Such a center would work closely with, and reinforce, existing institutions and initiatives in order to maximize the impact of the work and contribute to filling gaps where they exist.

Appendix

Statistics for 360 Weavers

Age

37/360 = 10% of the weavers are 20 years or younger

167/360 = 46% of the weavers are aged between 21 to 30 years

78/360 = 22% of the weavers are aged between 31 to 40 years

58/360 = 16% of the weavers are aged 41 to 50 years

22/360 = 6% of the weavers are above 50 years old

Marriage

195/360 = 54% of the weavers are married

138/360 = 38% of the weavers are single

23/360 = 6% of the weavers are widows

4/360 = 1% of the weavers are divorced

Children

216/360 = 60% of the weavers have children

144/360 = 40% of the weavers do not have children

790/216: The average number of children per family is 4.

Level of Education

56/360 = 15.5% of the weavers never had any formal education

154/360 = 43% of the weavers did not finish their primary school

150/360 = 42% of the weavers finished their primary school education, but did not complete their high school education

Employment

85.55% (308) of the 360 respondents gained employment as a result of weaving and joining weaving associations. They were previously subsistence farmers.

Education

A total of 272 children are currently attending primary school. 79% (214) are being paid for by parents from the fees they earn from weaving.

A total of 45 children are currently attending high school. 20% (9) of these are being paid for by parents who earn fees from weaving.

Source of Income

Before weaving, only 2% (8) of the 360 weavers had small businesses;

23% (82) were earning money from agriculture;

75% (271) had no source of income.

Living Standards

The weavers use their money on a range of different things:

62% said they use they money to buy food;

43% have bought animals;

33% have been able to rent land from their earnings;

22% have managed to pay for their children's school fees;

13.05% have been able to buy land;

3.33% have been able to build their own houses.

Diet

10.83% of the weavers have not changed their diet;

75.27% eat more than they used to previously;

2.22% eat more fruit than before;

26.38% eat more meat than they used to; and

8.33% drink more milk than before.

Weaving and Other Income-Generating Activities

56.38% (203) of the 360 weavers want to focus exclusively on weaving. 39.44% (142) of the weavers are interested in other income-generating activities to support their weaving. 3.1% (11) would like to leave weaving for other income-generating activities and 1.11% (4) would like to leave weaving and continue studying.

Medical Insurance

86.66% (312) have medical insurance; 52.56% (164) of the 312 obtained medical insurance since they became weavers. 13.33% (48) do not yet have medical insurance.

Saving Scheme

37.5% (135) have joined a saving scheme; 66.66% (90) of the 135 opened personal bank accounts since they became weavers.

HIV and AIDS

59% (214) of the weavers have been tested for HIV/AIDS;

41% (146) have not been tested for HIV/AIDS;

91% (133) of the 146 would like to be tested for HIV/AIDS;

9% (13) of the 146 do not want to be tested because they fear positive results, or because they are confident that they are HIV-negative.

On the Making of the Baskets

8 days is the average time it takes a weaver to complete a basket;

3 baskets is the average number of baskets made in a month;

On average a weaver earns 6720 Rwandese francs per basket, and spends 1068 francs to make a basket;

The maximum a weaver makes in a month is 32,000 francs;

The minimum a weaver makes in a month is 6000 francs, and the average is 17,395 francs in month.